Love Poems

Love Poems

Word Cloud Classics
San Diego

© 2019 Canterbury Classics

Canterbury Classics
An imprint of Printers Row Publishing Group
10350 Barnes Canyon Road, Suite 100, San Diego, CA 92121
www.canterburyclassicsbooks.com

Printers Row Publishing Group is a division of
Readerlink Distribution Services, LLC.
The Canterbury Classics and Word Cloud Classics names and logos
are registered trademarks of Readerlink Distribution Services, LLC.

All correspondence concerning the content of this book should be addressed to
Canterbury Classics, Editorial Department, at the above address.

Publisher: Peter Norton
Associate Publisher: Ana Parker
Publishing/Editorial Team: April Farr, Kelly Larsen, Kathryn C. Dalby
Editorial Team: JoAnn Padgett, Melinda Allman, Dan Mansfield
Production Team: Jonathan Lopes, Rusty von Dyl
Cover and endpaper design: Ray Caramanna

Library of Congress Cataloging-in-Publication Data available on request.

ISBN: 978-1-68412-993-5

Printed in China

23 22 21 20 19 1 2 3 4 5

*Editor's Note: These works have been published in their original form
to preserve the authors' intent and style.*

CONTENTS

Percy Bysshe Shelley

John Keats

Charles Swain

Elizabeth Barrett Browning

JAMES WHITCOMB RILEY

OSCAR WILDE

PAKENHAM BEATTY

SAPPHO
(c. 630–570 BC)

TRANSLATED BY JOHN MYERS O'HARA (1910)

Passion

Now Love shakes my soul, a mighty
  Wind from the high mountain falling
  Full on the oaks of the forest;

Now, limb-relaxing, it masters
  My life and implacable thrills me,
  Rending with anguish and rapture.

Now my heart, paining my bosom,
  Pants with desire as a mænad
  Mad for the orgiac revel.

Now under my skin run subtle
  Arrows of flame, and my body
  Quivers with surge of emotion.

Now long importunate yearnings
  Vanquish with surfeit my reason;
  Fainting my senses forsake me.

The First Kiss

And down I set the cushion
Upon the couch that she,
Relaxed supine upon it,
Might give her lips to me.

As some enamored priestess
At Aphrodite's shrine,
Entranced I bent above her
With sense of the divine.

She had, by nature nubile,
In years a child, no hint
Of any secret knowledge
Of passion's least intent.

Her mouth for immolation
Was ripe, and mine the art;
And one long kiss of passion
Deflowered her virgin heart.

Comparison

Less soft a Tyrian robe
　Of texture fine,
Less delicate a rose
　Than flesh of thine.

Whiter thy breast than snow
　That virgin lies,
And deeper than the blue
　Of seas thy eyes.

More golden than the fruit
　Of orange trees,
Thy locks that floating lure
　The satyr breeze.

Less fine of silver string
　An Orphic lyre,
Less sweet than thy low laugh
　That wakes desire.

HENRY HOWARD, EARL OF SURREY
(c. 1517–1547)

Give Place, Ye Lovers

Give place, ye lovers, here before
   That spent your boasts and brags in vain;
My lady's beauty passeth more
   The best of yours, I dare well sayen,
Than doth the sun the candle light,
Or brightest day the darkest night.

And thereto hath a troth as just
   As had Penelope the fair;
For what she saith, ye may it trust,
   As it by writing sealèd were:
And virtues hath she many mo'
Than I with pen have skill to show.

I could rehearse, if that I would,
   The whole effect of Nature's plaint,
When she had lost the perfect mould,
   The like to whom she could not paint:
With wringing hands, how she did cry,
And what she said, I know it aye.

I know she swore with raging mind,
   Her kingdom only set apart,
There was no loss by law of kind
   That could have gone so near her heart;

And this was chiefly all her pain;
"She could not make the like again."

Sith Nature thus gave her the praise,
　To be the chiefest work she wrought,
In faith, methink, some better ways
　On your behalf might well be sought,
Than to compare, as ye have done,
To match the candle with the sun.

SIR WALTER RALEIGH
(c. 1552–1618)

The Nymph's Reply

WRITTEN IN RESPONSE TO CHRISTOPHER MARLOWE'S
"THE PASSIONATE SHEPHERD TO HIS LOVE" (PAGE 10)

If all the world and love were young,
And truth in every Shepherd's tongue,
These pretty pleasures might me move
To live with thee, and be thy love.

Time drives the flocks from field to fold,
When rivers rage and rocks grow cold;
And Philomel becometh dumb,
The rest complains of cares to come.

The flowers do fade, and wanton fields
To wayward winter reckoning yields;
A honey tongue, a heart of gall,
Is fancy's spring, but sorrow's fall.

Thy gown, thy shoes, thy beds of roses,
Thy cap, the kirtle, and thy posies,
Soon break, soon wither, soon forgotten,
In folly ripe, in reason rotten.

Thy belt of straw and ivy buds,
Thy coral clasps and amber studs;

All these in me no means can move
To come to thee and be thy love.

But could youth last, and love still breed,
Had joys no date, nor age no need,
Then these delights my mind might move
To live with thee and be thy love.

ROBERT GREENE
(1558–1592)

Philomela's Ode

THAT SHE SUNG IN HER ARBOR

Sitting by a river's side
Where a silent stream did glide,
Muse I did of many things
That the mind in quiet brings.
I 'gan think how some men deem
Gold their god; and some esteem
Honor is the chief content
That to man in life is lent;
And some others do contend
Quiet none like to a friend.
Others hold there is no wealth
Compared to a perfect health;
Some man's mind in quiet stands
When he 's lord of many lands.
But I did sigh, and said all this
Was but a shade of perfect bliss:
And in my thoughts I did approve
Naught so sweet as is true love.
Love 'twixt lovers passeth these,
When mouth kisseth and heart 'grees—
With folded arms and lips meeting,
Each soul another sweetly greeting;
For by the breath the soul fleeteth,
And soul with soul in kissing meeteth.

If love be so sweet a thing,
That such happy bliss doth bring,
Happy is love's sugared thrall;
But unhappy maidens all
Who esteem your virgin blisses
Sweeter than a wife's sweet kisses.
No such quiet to the mind
As true love with kisses kind;
But if a kiss prove unchaste,
Then is true love quite disgraced.
Though love be sweet, learn this of me,
No sweet love but honesty.

CHRISTOPHER MARLOWE
(1564–1593)

Love

From HERO AND LEANDER

It lies not in our power to love or hate,
For will in us is over-ruled by fate.
When two are stript long e'er the course begin,
We wish that one should lose, the other win;
And one especially do we affect
Of two gold ingots, like in each respect:
The reason no man knows; let it suffice,
What we behold is censured by our eyes.
Where both deliberate, the love is slight:
Who ever loved, that loved not at first sight?

The Passionate Shepherd to His Love

Come live with me and be my Love,
And we will all the pleasures prove,
That hills and valleys, dales and fields,
Woods or steepy mountains yield.

And we will sit upon the rocks,
And see the shepherds feed their flocks
By shallow rivers, to whose falls
Melodious birds sing madrigals.

And will I make thee beds of roses,
And a thousand fragrant posies;
A cap of flowers and a kirtle
Embroidered all with leaves of myrtle;

A gown made of the finest wool
Which from our pretty lambs we pull;
Fair-linèd slippers for the cold,
With buckles of the purest gold;

A belt of straw and ivy buds,
With coral clasps and amber studs:
And if these pleasures may thee move,
Come live with me, and be my Love.

The shepherd swains shall dance and sing
For thy delight each May morning;
If these delights thy mind may move,
Then live with me, and be my Love.

WILLIAM SHAKESPEARE
(1564–1616)

Sonnet 2

When forty winters shall besiege thy brow,
And dig deep trenches in thy beauty's field,
Thy youth's proud livery, so gazed on now,
Will be a tatter'd weed, of small worth held:
Then being ask'd where all thy beauty lies,
Where all the treasure of thy lusty days;
To say, within thine own deep-sunken eyes,
Were an all-eating shame and thriftless praise.
How much more praise deserved thy beauty's use,
If thou couldst answer, "This fair child of mine
Shall sum my count, and make my old excuse,"
Proving his beauty by succession thine!
    This were to be new made when thou art old,
    And see thy blood warm when thou feel'st it cold.

Sonnet 18

Shall I compare thee to a summer's day?
Thou art more lovely and more temperate:
Rough winds do shake the darling buds of May,
And summer's lease hath all too short a date:
Sometime too hot the eye of heaven shines,
And often is his gold complexion dimm'd;
And every fair from fair sometime declines,
By chance, or nature's changing course, untrimm'd;
But thy eternal summer shall not fade,

Nor lose possession of that fair thou ow'st;
Nor shall Death brag thou wander'st in his shade,
When in eternal lines to time thou grow'st:
    So long as men can breathe, or eyes can see,
    So long lives this, and this gives life to thee.

Sonnet 40

Take all my loves, my love, yea, take them all;
What hast thou then more than thou hadst before?
No love, my love, that thou mayst true love call;
All mine was thine before thou hadst this more.
Then, if for my love thou my love receivest,
I cannot blame thee for my love thou usest;
But yet be blamed, if thou this self deceivest
By wilful taste of what thyself refusest.
I do forgive thy robbery, gentle thief,
Although thou steal thee all my poverty;
And yet, love knows, it is a greater grief
To bear love's wrong than hate's known injury.
    Lascivious grace, in whom all ill well shows,
    Kill me with spites; yet we must not be foes.

Sonnet 43

When most I wink, then do mine eyes best see,
For all the day they view things unrespected;
But when I sleep, in dreams they look on thee,
And, darkly bright, are bright in dark directed.
Then thou, whose shadow shadows doth make bright,
How would thy shadow's form form happy show

To the clear day with thy much clearer light,
When to unseeing eyes thy shade shines so!
How would (I say) mine eyes be blessèd made
By looking on thee in the living day,
When in dead night thy fair imperfect shade
Through heavy sleep on sightless eyes doth stay!
    All days are nights to see till I see thee,
    And nights bright days when dreams do show thee me.

Sonnet 55

Not marble, nor the gilded monuments
Of princes, shall outlive this powerful rime;
But you shall shine more bright in these contents
Than unswept stone, besmear'd with sluttish time.
When wasteful war shall statues overturn,
And broils root out the work of masonry,
Nor Mars his sword nor war's quick fire shall burn
The living record of your memory.
'Gainst death, and all-oblivious enmity
Shall you pace forth; your praise shall still find room
Even in the eyes of all posterity
That wear this world out to the ending doom.
    So, till the judgement that yourself arise,
    You live in this, and dwell in lovers' eyes.

Sonnet 56

Sweet love, renew thy force; be it not said
Thy edge should blunter be than appetite,
Which but to-day by feeding is allay'd,

To-morrow sharpen'd in his former might:
So, love, be thou; although to-day thou fill
Thy hungry eyes even till they wink with fullness,
To-morrow see again, and do not kill
The spirit of love with a perpetual dullness.
Let this sad interim like the ocean be
Which parts the shore, where two contracted new
Come daily to the banks, that when they see
Return of love, more bless'd may be the view;
   Or call it winter, which being full of care,
   Makes summer's welcome thrice more wish'd, more rare.

Sonnet 57

Being your slave, what should I do but tend
Upon the hours and times of your desire?
I have no precious time at all to spend,
Nor services to do, till you require.
Nor dare I chide the world-without-end hour
Whilst I, my sovereign, watch the clock for you,
Nor think the bitterness of absence sour,
When you have bid your servant once adieu;
Nor dare I question with my jealous thought
Where you may be, or your affairs suppose,
But, like a sad slave, stay and think of nought
Save, where you are how happy you make those.
   So true a fool is love, that in your will,
   Though you do any thing, he thinks no ill.

Sonnet 58

That god forbid that made me first your slave,
I should in thought control your times of pleasure,
Or at your hand the account of hours to crave,
Being your vassal, bound to stay your leisure!
O, let me suffer, being at your beck,
The imprison'd absence of your liberty;
And patience, tame to sufferance, bide each check,
Without accusing you of injury.
Be where you list, your charter is so strong,
That you yourself may privilege your time
To what you will; to you it doth belong
Yourself to pardon of self-doing crime.
    I am to wait, though waiting so be hell;
    Not blame your pleasure, be it ill or well.

Sonnet 61

Is it thy will thy image should keep open
My heavy eyelids to the weary night?
Dost thou desire my slumbers should be broken,
While shadows like to thee do mock my sight?
Is it thy spirit that thou send'st from thee
So far from home into my deeds to pry,
To find out shames and idle hours in me,
The scope and tenure of thy jealousy?
O, no! thy love, though much, is not so great:
It is my love that keeps mine eye awake:
Mine own true love that doth my rest defeat,
To play the watchman ever for thy sake:

For thee watch I whilst thou dost wake elsewhere,
From me far off, with others all too near.

Sonnet 73

That time of year thou mayst in me behold
When yellow leaves, or none, or few, do hang
Upon those boughs which shake against the cold,
Bare ruin'd choirs, where late the sweet birds sang.
In me thou see'st the twilight of such day
As after sunset fadeth in the west;
Which by and by black night doth take away,
Death's second self, that seals up all in rest.
In me thou see'st the glowing of such fire,
That on the ashes of his youth doth lie,
As the death-bed whereon it must expire,
Consum'd with that which it was nourisht by.
    This thou perceiv'st, which makes thy love more strong,
    To love that well which thou must leave ere long.

Sonnet 75

So are you to my thoughts as food to life,
Or as sweet-season'd showers are to the ground;
And for the peace of you I hold such strife
As 'twixt a miser and his wealth is found;
Now proud as an enjoyer, and anon
Doubting the filching age will steal his treasure;
Now counting best to be with you alone,
Then better'd that the world may see my pleasure:
Sometime all full with feasting on your sight,

And by and by clean starved for a look;
Possessing or pursuing no delight,
Save what is had or must from you be took.
    Thus do I pine and surfeit day by day,
    Or gluttoning on all, or all away.

Sonnet 91

Some glory in their birth, some in their skill,
Some in their wealth, some in their bodies' force;
Some in their garments, though new-fangled ill;
Some in their hawks and hounds, some in their horse;
And every humour hath his adjunct pleasure,
Wherein it finds a joy above the rest:
But these particulars are not my measure;
All these I better in one general best.
Thy love is better than high birth to me,
Richer than wealth, prouder than garments' cost,
Of more delight than hawks or horses be;
And having thee, of all men's pride I boast:
    Wretched in this alone, that thou mayst take
    All this away, and me most wretchced make.

Sonnet 97

How like a winter hath my absence been
From thee, the pleasure of the fleeting year!
What freezings have I felt, what dark days seen!
What old December's bareness every where!
And yet this time remov'd was summer's time;
The teeming autumn, big with rich increase,

Bearing the wanton burden of the prime,
Like widow'd wombs after their lords' decease:
Yet this abundant issue seem'd to me
But hope of orphans and unfather'd fruit;
For summer and his pleasures wait on thee,
And, thou away, the very birds are mute;
    Or, if they sing, 'tis with so dull a cheer,
    That leaves look pale, dreading the winter's near.

Sonnet 98

From you have I been absent in the spring,
When proud-pied April, dress'd in all his trim,
Hath put a spirit of youth in every thing,
That heavy Saturn laugh'd and leap'd with him.
Yet nor the lays of birds, nor the sweet smell
Of different flowers in odour and in hue,
Could make me any summer's story tell,
Or from their proud lap pluck them where they grew:
Nor did I wonder at the lily's white,
Nor praise the deep vermilion in the rose;
They were but sweet, but figures of delight,
Drawn after you,—you pattern of all those.
    Yet seem'd it winter still, and, you away,
    As with your shadow I with these did play.

Sonnet 105

Let not my love be call'd idolatry,
Nor my beloved as an idol show,
Since all alike my songs and praises be

To one, of one, still such, and ever so.
Kind is my love to-day, to-morrow kind,
Still constant in a wondrous excellence;
Therefore my verse to constancy confin'd,
One thing expressing, leaves out difference.
Fair, kind, and true, is all my argument,—
Fair, kind, and true, varying to other words;
And in this change is my invention spent,
Three themes in one, which wondrous scope affords.
    Fair, kind, and true, have often lived alone,
    Which three till now never kept seat in one.

Sonnet 109

O, never say that I was false of heart,
Though absence seem'd my flame to qualify.
As easy might I from myself depart
As from my soul, which in thy breast doth lie:
That is my home of love: if I have rang'd,
Like him that travels I return again,
Just to the time, not with the time exchang'd,
So that myself bring water for my stain.
Never believe, though in my nature reign'd
All frailties that besiege all kinds of blood,
That it could so preposterously be stain'd,
To leave for nothing all thy sum of good;
    For nothing this wide universe I call,
    Save thou, my rose; in it thou art my all.

Sonnet 116

Let me not to the marriage of true minds
Admit impediments. Love is not love
Which alters when it alteration finds,
Or bends with the remover to remove:
O, no! it is an ever-fixed mark,
That looks on tempests and is never shaken,
It is the star to every wandering bark,
Whose worth's unknown, although his height be taken.
Love's not Time's fool, though rosy lips and cheeks
Within his bending sickle's compass come;
Love alters not with his brief hours and weeks,
But bears it out even to the edge of doom.
    If this be error, and upon me prov'd,
    I never writ, nor no man ever lov'd.

Sonnet 130

My mistress' eyes are nothing like the sun;
Coral is far more red than her lips' red:
If snow be white, why then her breasts are dun;
If hairs be wires, black wires grow on her head.
I have seen roses damask'd, red and white,
But no such roses see I in her cheeks;
And in some perfumes is there more delight
Than in the breath that from my mistress reeks.
I love to hear her speak, yet well I know
That music hath a far more pleasing sound:
I grant I never saw a goddess go;
My mistress, when she walks, treads on the ground.

And yet, by heaven, I think my love as rare
As any she belied with false compare.

Sonnet 147

My love is as a fever, longing still
For that which longer nurseth the disease;
Feeding on that which doth preserve the ill,
The uncertain sickly appetite to please.
My reason, the physician to my love,
Angry that his prescriptions are not kept,
Hath left me, and I desperate now approve
Desire is death, which physic did except.
Past cure I am, now Reason is past care,
And frantic-mad with evermore unrest;
My thoughts and my discourse as madmen's are,
At random from the truth vainly exprest;
    For I have sworn thee fair, and thought thee bright,
    Who art as black as hell, as dark as night.

Sonnet 148

O me, what eyes hath Love put in my head,
Which have no correspondence with true sight!
Or, if they have, where is my judgement fled,
That censures falsely what they see aright?
If that be fair whereon my false eyes dote,
What means the world to say it is not so?
If it be not, then love doth well denote
Love's eye is not so true as all men's: no.
How can it? O, how can Love's eye be true,

That is so vex'd with watching and with tears?
No marvel, then, though I mistake my view;
The sun itself sees not till heaven clears.
    O cunning Love! with tears thou keep'st me blind,
    Lest eyes well-seeing thy foul faults should find.

Who Is Silvia?

From THE TWO GENTLEMEN OF VERONA

Who is Silvia? What is she,
    That all our swains commend her?
Holy, fair, and wise is she;
    The heaven such grace did lend her,
That she might admired be.

    Is she kind as she is fair?
For beauty lives with kindness.
    Love doth to her eyes repair,
To help him of his blindness;
    And, being help'd, inhabits there.

Then to Silvia let us sing
    That Silvia is excelling;
She excels each mortal thing
    Upon the dull earth dwelling.
To her let us garlands bring.

It Was a Lover and His Lass

From AS YOU LIKE IT

It was a lover and his lass,
    With a hey, and a ho, and a hey nonino,
That o'er the green corn-field did pass
    In the spring time, the only pretty ring time,
When birds do sing, hey ding a ding, ding:
Sweet lovers love the spring.

Between the acres of the rye,
    With a hey, and a ho, and a hey nonino,
These pretty country folks would lie,
    In the spring time, the only pretty ring time,
When birds do sing, hey ding a ding, ding:
Sweet lovers love the spring.

This carol they began that hour,
    With a hey, and a ho, and a hey nonino,
How that a life was but a flower,
    In the spring time, the only pretty ring time,
When birds do sing, hey ding a ding, ding:
Sweet lovers love the spring.

And therefore take the present time,
    With a hey, and a ho, and a hey nonino,
For love is crown'd with the prime,
    In the spring time, the only pretty ring time,
When birds do sing, hey ding a ding, ding:
Sweet lovers love the spring.

O, *Mistress Mine*

From Twelfth Night

O, mistress mine, where are you roaming?
O, stay and hear; your true love's coming,
    That can sing both high and low;
Trip no further, pretty sweeting,
Journeys end in lovers meeting—
    Every wise man's son doth know.

What is love? 'tis not hereafter;
Present mirth hath present laughter;
    What's to come is still unsure.
In delay there lies no plenty—
Then come kiss me, sweet and twenty;
    Youth's a stuff will not endure.

SIR HENRY WOTTON

(1568–1639)

Elizabeth, Queen of Bohemia

You meaner beauties of the night,
　That poorly satisfy our eyes
More by your number than your light,
　You common people of the skies;
What are you when the moon shall rise?

You curious chanters of the wood,
　That warble forth Dame Nature's lays,
Thinking your passions understood
　By your weak accents; what's your praise
When Philomel her voice shall raise?

You violets that first appear,
　By your pure purple mantles known
Like the proud virgins of the year,
　As if the spring were all your own;
What are you when the rose is blown?

So, when my mistress shall be seen
　In form and beauty of her mind,
By virtue first, then choice, a Queen,
　Tell me, if she were not designed
Th' eclipse and glory of her kind.

BEN JONSON
(1572–1637)

Song: To Celia

Drink to me only with thine eyes,
　　And I will pledge with mine;
Or leave a kiss but in the cup,
　　And I'll not look for wine.
The thirst that from the soul doth rise
　　Doth ask a drink divine;
But might I of Jove's nectar sup,
　　I would not change for thine.

I sent thee late a rosy wreath,
　　Not so much honouring thee
As giving it a hope, that there
　　It could not withered be.
But thou thereon didst only breathe,
　　And sent'st it back to me;
Since when it grows, and smells, I swear,
　　Not of itself, but thee.

The Triumph of Charis

See the chariot at hand here of Love,
　Wherein my lady rideth!
Each that draws is a swan or a dove,
　And well the car Love guideth.
As she goes, all hearts do duty
　　Unto her beauty;

And enamour'd, do wish, so they might
    But enjoy such a sight,
That they still were to run by her side,
Through swords, through seas, whither she
    would ride.

Do but look on her eyes, they do light
    All that Love's world compriseth!
Do but look on her hair, it is bright
    As Love's star when it riseth!
Do but mark, her forehead's smoother
    Than words that soothe her;
And from her arched brows, such a grace
    Sheds itself through the face
As alone there triumphs to the life
All the gain, all the good, of the elements'
    strife.

Have you seen but a bright lily grow,
    Before rude hands have touch'd it?
Ha' you mark'd but the fall o' the snow
    Before the soil hath smutch'd it?
Ha' you felt the wool o' the beaver?
    Or swan's down ever?
Or have smelt o' the bud o' the brier?
    Or the nard in the fire?
Or have tasted the bag of the bee?
Oh so white! Oh so soft! Oh so sweet is she!

ROBERT HERRICK
(1591–1674)

To Dianeme

Sweet, be not proud of those two eyes,
Which star-like sparkle in their skies;
Nor be you proud, that you can see
All hearts your captives, yours, yet free;
Be you not proud of that rich hair
Which wantons with the love-sick air;
Whenas that ruby which you wear,
Sunk from the tip of your soft ear,
Will last to be a precious stone,
When all your world of beauty's gone.

THOMAS CAREW
(1595–1640)

Disdain Returned

He that loves a rosy cheek,
  Or a coral lip admires,
Or from star-like eyes doth seek
  Fuel to maintain his fires;
As old Time makes these decay,
So his flames must waste away.

But a smooth and steadfast mind,
  Gentle thoughts and calm desires,
Hearts with equal love combin'd,
  Kindle never-dying fires.
Where these are not, I despise
Lovely cheeks, or lips, or eyes.

No tears, Celia, now shall win
  My resolv'd heart to return;
I have search'd thy soul within,
  And find nought, but pride, and scorn;
I have learn'd thy arts, and now
Can disdain as much as thou.
Some power, in my revenge, convey
That love to her I cast away.

WILLIAM STRODE
(c. 1602–1645)

Kisses

My love and I for kisses played:
   She would keep stakes—I was content;
But when I won, she would be paid;
   This made me ask her what she meant.
"Pray since I see," quoth she, "your wrangling vein,
Take your own kisses; give me mine again."

THOMAS RANDOLPH
(1605–1635)

Admiration

TO A LADY ADMIRING HERSELF IN A LOOKING-GLASS

Fair lady, when you see the grace
Of beauty in your looking-glass;
A stately forehead, smooth and high,
And full of princely majesty;
A sparkling eye no gem so fair,
Whose lustre dims the Cyprian star;
A glorious cheek, divinely sweet,
Wherein both roses kindly meet;
A cherry lip that would entice
Even gods to kiss at any price;
You think no beauty is so rare
That with your shadow might compare;
That your reflection is alone
The thing that men most dote upon.
Madam, alas! your glass doth lie,
And you are much deceived; for I
A beauty know of richer grace
(Sweet, be not angry), 't is your face.
Hence, then, O, learn more mild to be,
And leave to lay your blame on me:
If me your real substance move,
When you so much your shadow love,
Wise nature would not let your eye
Look on her own bright majesty;

Which, had you once but gazed upon,
You could, except yourself, love none:
What then you cannot love, let me,
That face I can, you cannot see.
  Now you have what to love, you'll say,
What then is left for me, I pray?
My face, sweet heart, if it please thee;
That which you can, I cannot see,
So either love shall gain his due,
Yours, sweet, in me, and mine in you.

SIR JOHN SUCKLING
(1609–1641)

Why So Pale and Wan?

Why so pale and wan, fond lover?
   Prithee, why so pale?
Will, when looking well can't move her,
   Looking ill prevail?
   Prithee, why so pale?

Why so dull and mute, young sinner?
   Prithee, why so mute?
Will, when speaking well can't win her,
   Saying nothing do't?
   Prithee, why so mute?

Quit, quit, for shame! this will not move,
   This cannot take her:
If of herself she will not love,
   Nothing can make her:
   The devil take her!

JOHN DRYDEN
(1631–1700)

You Charm'd Me Not with That Fair Face

From AN EVENING'S LOVE

You charm'd me not with that fair face
    Though it was all divine:
To be another's is the grace,
    That makes me wish you mine.

The Gods and Fortune take their part
    Who like young monarchs fight;
And boldly dare invade that heart
    Which is another's right.

First mad with hope we undertake
    To pull up every bar;
But once possess'd, we faintly make
    A dull defensive war.

Now every friend is turn'd a foe
    In hope to get our store:
And passion makes us cowards grow,
    Which made us brave before.

Ah, How Sweet It Is to Love

From TYRANNIC LOVE

Ah, how sweet it is to love!
  Ah, how gay is young desire!
And what pleasing pains we prove
  When we first approach love's fire!
Pains of love be sweeter far
Than all other pleasures are.

Sighs which are from lovers blown
  Do but gently heave the heart:
E'en the tears they shed alone
  Cure, like trickling balm, their smart.
Lovers, when they lose their breath,
Bleed away in easy death.

Love and Time with reverence use,
  Treat them like a parting friend;
Nor the golden gifts refuse
  Which in youth sincere they send:
For each year their price is more,
And they less simple than before.

Love, like spring-tides full and high,
  Swells in every youthful vein;
But each tide does less supply,
  Till they quite shrink in again.
If a flow in age appear,
  'T is but rain, and runs not clear.

GEORGE ETHEREGE
(1636–1692)

Sylvia

The Nymph that undoes me, is fair and unkind;
No less than a wonder by Nature designed.
She's the grief of my heart, the joy of my eye;
And the cause of a flame that never can die!

Her mouth, from whence wit still obligingly flows,
Has the beautiful blush, and the smell, of the rose.
Love and Destiny both attend on her will;
She wounds with a look; with a frown, she can kill!

The desperate Lover can hope no redress;
Where Beauty and Rigour are both in excess!
In Sylvia they meet; so unhappy am I!
Who sees her, must love; and who loves her, must die!

ALEXANDER POPE
(1688–1744)

Belinda

From THE RAPE OF THE LOCK

On her white breast a sparkling cross she wore,
Which Jews might kiss, and Infidels adore.
Her lively looks a sprightly mind disclose,
Quick as her eyes, and as unfix'd as those:
Favours to none, to all she smiles extends;
Oft she rejects, but never once offends.
Bright as the sun, her eyes the gazers strike,
And, like the sun, they shine on all alike.
Yet graceful ease, and sweetness void of pride,
Might hide her faults, if belles had faults to hide:
If to her share some female errors fall,
Look on her face, and you'll forget them all.

OLIVER GOLDSMITH
(1728–1774)

The Hermit

From THE VICAR OF WAKEFIELD

"Turn, gentle Hermit of the dale,
  And guide my lonely way
To where yon taper cheers the vale
  With hospitable ray.

"For here forlorn and lost I tread,
  With fainting steps and slow;
Where wilds, immeasurably spread,
  Seem lengthening as I go."

"Forbear, my son," the Hermit cries,
  "To tempt the dangerous gloom;
For yonder faithless phantom flies
  To lure thee to thy doom.

"Here to the houseless child of want
  My door is open still;
And though my portion is but scant,
  I give it with good will.

"Then turn to-night, and freely share
  Whate'er my cell bestows;
My rushy couch and frugal fare,
  My blessing and repose.

"No flocks that range the valley free
  To slaughter I condemn;
Taught by that Power that pities me,
  I learn to pity them:

"But from the mountain's grassy side
  A guiltless feast I bring;
A scrip with herbs and fruits supplied,
  And water from the spring.

"Then, pilgrim, turn, thy cares forego;
  All earth-born cares are wrong:
Man wants but little here below,
  Nor wants that little long."

Soft as the dew from heaven descends,
  His gentle accents fell:
The modest stranger lowly bends,
  And follows to the cell.

Far in a wilderness obscure
  The lonely mansion lay;
A refuge to the neighboring poor,
  And strangers led astray.

No stores beneath its humble thatch
  Required a master's care:
The wicket, opening with a latch,
  Received the harmless pair.

And now, when busy crowds retire
  To take their evening rest,
The Hermit trimmed his little fire,
  And cheered his pensive guest;

And spread his vegetable store,
  And gayly pressed and smiled;
And, skilled in legendary lore,
  The lingering hours beguiled.

Around, in sympathetic mirth,
  Its tricks the kitten tries;
The cricket chirrups on the hearth;
  The crackling fagot flies.

But nothing could a charm impart
  To soothe the stranger's woe;
For grief was heavy at his heart,
  And tears began to flow.

His rising cares the Hermit spied,
  With answering care opprest:
"And whence, unhappy youth," he cried,
  "The sorrows of thy breast?

"From better habitations spurned,
  Reluctant dost thou rove"
Or grieve for friendship unreturned,
  Or unregarded love?

"Alas! the joys that fortune brings
  Are trifling, and decay;
And those who prize the paltry things
  More trifling still than they.

"And what is friendship but a name,
  A charm that lulls to sleep;
A shade that follows wealth or fame,
  And leaves the wretch to weep?

"And love is still an emptier sound,
  The modern fair one's jest;
On earth unseen, or only found
  To warm the turtle's nest.

"For shame, fond youth! thy sorrows hush,
  And spurn the sex," he said;
But while he spoke, a rising blush
  His lovelorn guest betrayed.

Surprised, he sees new beauties rise,
  Swift mantling to the view;
Like colors o'er the morning skies,
  As bright, as transient too.

The bashful look, the rising breast,
  Alternate spread alarms:
The lovely stranger stands confest
  A maid in all her charms.

"And, ah! forgive a stranger rude,
　A wretch forlorn," she cried;
"Whose feet unhallowed thus intrude
　Where heaven and you reside.

"But let a maid thy pity share,
　Whom love has taught to stray;
Who seeks for rest, but finds despair
　Companion of her way.

"My father lived beside the Tyne,
　A wealthy lord was he;
And all his wealth was marked as mine,"
　He had but only me.

"To win me from his tender arms,
　Unnumbered suitors came;
Who praised me for imputed charms,
　And felt, or feigned, a flame.

"Each hour a mercenary crowd
　With richest proffers strove:
Among the rest young Edwin bowed,
　But never talked of love.

"In humble, simplest habit clad,
　No wealth or power had he;
Wisdom and worth were all he had,
　But these were all to me.

"And when beside me in the dale
  He carolled lays of love,
 His breath lent fragrance to the gale
  And music to the grove.

"The blossom opening to the day,
  The dews of heaven refined,
 Could naught of purity display
  To emulate his mind.

"The dew, the blossoms of the tree,
  With charms inconstant shine;
 Their charms were his, but, woe to me!
  Their constancy was mine.

"For still I tried each fickle art,
  Importunate and vain;
 And while his passion touched my heart,
  I triumphed in his pain:

"Till, quite dejected with my scorn,
  He left me to my pride;
 And sought a solitude forlorn,
  In secret, where he died.

"But mine the sorrow, mine the fault,
  And well my life shall pay;
 I'll seek the solitude he sought,
  And stretch me where he lay.

"And there forlorn, despairing, hid,
　I'll lay me down and die;
'T was so for me that Edwin did,
　And so for him will I."

"Forbid it, Heaven!" the Hermit cried,
　And clasped her to his breast:
The wondering fair one turned to chide—
　'T was Edwin's self that pressed.

"Turn, Angelina, ever dear,
　My charmer, turn to see
Thy own, thy long-lost Edwin here,
　Restored to love and thee.

"Thus let me hold thee to my heart,
　And every care resign:
And shall we never, never part,
　My life—my all that's mine?"

"No, never from this hour to part,
　We'll live and love so true:
The sigh that rends thy constant heart
　Shall break thy Edwin's too."

THOMAS CHATTERTON
(1752–1770)

Minstrels' Marriage Song

From AELLA: A TRAGICAL INTERLUDE

FIRST MINSTREL

The budding floweret blushes at the light:
  The meads are sprinkled with the yellow hue;
In daisied mantles is the mountain dight;
  The slim young cowslip bendeth with the dew;
The trees enleafèd, into heaven straught,
When gentle winds do blow, to whistling din are
    brought.

The evening comes and brings the dew along;
  The ruddy welkin sheeneth to the eyne;
Around the ale-stake minstrels sing the song;
  Young ivy round the doorpost doth entwine;
I lay me on the grass; yet, to my will,
Albeit all is fair, there lacketh something still.

SECOND MINSTREL

So Adam thought, what time, in Paradise,
  All heaven and earth did homage to his mind.
In woman and none else man's pleasaunce lies,
  As instruments of joy are kind with kind.
Go, take a wife unto thine arms, and see
Winter and dusky hills will have a charm for thee.

WILLIAM BLAKE
(1757–1827)

A Cradle Song

Sweet dreams, form a shade
O'er my lovely infant's head!
Sweet dreams of pleasant streams
By happy, silent, moony beams!

Sweet sleep, with soft down
Weave thy brows an infant crown!
Sweet sleep, angel mild,
Hover o'er my happy child!

Sweet smiles, in the night
Hover over my delight!
Sweet smiles, mother's smiles,
All the livelong night beguiles.

Sweet moans, dovelike sighs,
Chase not slumber from thy eyes!
Sweet moans, sweeter smiles,
All the dovelike moans beguiles.

Sleep, sleep, happy child!
All creation slept and smiled.
Sleep, sleep, happy sleep,
While o'er thee thy mother weep.

Sweet babe, in thy face
Holy image I can trace;
Sweet babe, once like thee
Thy Maker lay, and wept for me:

Wept for me, for thee, for all,
When He was an infant small.
Thou His image ever see,
Heavenly face that smiles on thee!

Smiles on thee, on me, on all,
Who became an infant small;
Infant smiles are His own smiles;
Heaven and earth to peace beguiles.

Love's Secret

Never seek to tell thy love,
Love that never told can be;
For the gentle wind does move
Silently, invisibly.

I told my love, I told my love,
I told her all my heart;
Trembling, cold, in ghastly fears,
Ah! she did depart!

Soon as she was gone from me,
A traveller came by,
Silently, invisibly,
He took her with a sigh.

The Clod and the Pebble

"Love seeketh not itself to please,
    Nor for itself hath any care,
But for another gives its ease,
    And builds a Heaven in Hell's despair."

So sung a little clod of clay,
    Trodden with the cattle's feet,
But a pebble of the brook
    Warbled out these metres meet:

"Love seeketh only Self to please,
    To bind another to its delight,
Joys in another's loss of ease,
    And builds a Hell in Heaven's despite."

ROBERT BURNS
(1759–1796)

A Red, Red Rose

O my Luve's like a red, red rose,
That's newly sprung in June:
O my Luve's like the melodie,
That's sweetly play'd in tune.

As fair art thou, my bonie lass,
So deep in luve am I;
And I will luve thee still, my dear,
Till a' the seas gang dry.

Till a' the seas gang dry, my dear,
And the rocks melt wi' the sun;
And I will luve thee still, my dear,
While the sands o' life shall run.

And fare-thee-weel, my only Luve!
And fare-thee-weel, a while!
And I will come again, my Luve,
Tho' 'twere ten thousand mile!

John Anderson, My Jo

John Anderson, my jo, John,
When we were first acquent;
Your locks were like the raven,
Your bonie brow was brent;

But now your brow is beld, John,
Your locks are like the snaw;
But blessings on your frosty pow,
John Anderson, my jo.

John Anderson, my jo, John,
We clamb the hill thegither;
And mony a cantie day, John,
We've had wi' ane anither:
Now we maun totter down, John,
And hand in hand we'll go,
And sleep thegither at the foot,
John Anderson, my jo.

Highland Mary

Ye banks and braes and streams around
The castle o' Montgomery!
Green be your woods, and fair your flowers,
Your waters never drumlie:
There Simmer first unfauld her robes,
And there the langest tarry;
For there I took the last Farewell
O' my sweet Highland Mary.

How sweetly bloom'd the gay green birk,
How rich the hawthorn's blossom,
As underneath their fragrant shade
I clasp'd her to my bosom!
The golden Hours on angel wings
Flew o'er me and my Dearie;

For dear to me as light and life
Was my sweet Highland Mary.

Wi' mony a vow and lock'd embrace,
Our parting was fu' tender;
And, pledging aft to meet again,
We tore oursels asunder;
But oh! fell Death's untimely frost,
That nipt my Flower sae early!
Now green's the sod, and cauld's the clay
That wraps my Highland Mary!

O pale, pale now, those rosy lips
I aft hae kiss'd sae fondly!
And clos'd for aye the sparkling glance
That dwalt on me sae kindly!
And mouldering now in silent dust,
That heart that lo'ed me dearly!
But still within my bosom's core
Shall live my Highland Mary.

Mary Morison

O Mary, at thy window be,
It is the wish'd, the trysted hour!
Those smiles and glances let me see,
That make the miser's treasure poor:
How blythely wad I bide the stour,
A weary slave frae sun to sun,
Could I the rich reward secure,
The lovely Mary Morison.

Yestreen, when to the trembling string
The dance gaed thro' the lighted ha',
To thee my fancy took its wing,
I sat, but neither heard nor saw:
Tho' this was fair, and that was braw,
And yon the toast of a' the town,
I sigh'd, and said among them a',
"Ye are na Mary Morison."

Oh, Mary, canst thou wreck his peace,
Wha for thy sake wad gladly die?
Or canst thou break that heart of his,
Whase only faut is loving thee?
If love for love thou wilt na gie,
At least be pity to me shown;
A thought ungentle canna be
The thought o' Mary Morison.

Let Not Woman E'er Complain

Let not woman e'er complain
    Of inconstancy in love;
Let not woman e'er complain
    Fickle man is apt to rove;
Look abroad through Nature's range,
Nature's mighty law is change;
Ladies, would it not be strange
    Man should then a monster prove?

Mark the winds, and mark the skies;
    Ocean's ebb and ocean's flow;

Sun and moon but set to rise,
  Round and round the seasons go.
Why then ask of silly man,
To oppose great Nature's plan?
We'll be constant while we can—
  You can be no more, you know.

Green Grow the Rashes, O

Green grow the rashes, O,
  Green grow the rashes, O;
The sweetest hours that e'er I spend
  Are spent amang the lasses, O!

There's nought but care on ev'ry han',
  In every hour that passes, O;
What signifies the life o' man,
  An' 'twere na for the lasses, O?

The war'ly race may riches chase,
  An' riches still may fly them, O;
An' though at last they catch them fast,
  Their hearts can ne'er enjoy them, O!

Gie me a canny hour at e'en,
  My arms about my dearie, O,
An' war'ly cares an' warly men
  May all gae tapsalteerie, O!

For you sae douce, ye sneer at this,
  Ye're nought but senseless asses, O;

The wisest man the warl' e'er saw
  He dearly lo'ed the lasses, O!

Auld Nature swears the lovely dears
  Her noblest work she classes, O:
Her 'prentice han' she tried on man,
  An' then she made the lasses, O!

O Whistle, and I'll Come to Ye, My Lad

O whistle, and I'll come to ye, my lad,
O whistle, and I'll come to ye, my lad,
Tho' father and mither and a' should gae mad,
O whistle, and I'll come to ye, my lad.

But warily tent, when ye come to court me,
And come na unless the back-yett be a-jee;
Syne up the back stile, and let naebody see,
And come as ye were na comin' to me.
And come as ye were na comin' to me.

O whistle, and I'll come to ye, my lad,
O whistle, and I'll come to ye, my lad,
Tho' father and mither and a' should gae mad,
O whistle, and I'll come to ye, my lad.

At kirk, or at market, whene'er ye meet me,
Gang by me as tho' that ye cared nae a flie;
But steal me a blink o' your bonnie black e'e,
Yet look as ye were na lookin' at me.
Yet look as ye were na lookin' at me.

O whistle, and I'll come to ye, my lad,
O whistle, and I'll come to ye, my lad,
Tho' father and mither and a' should gae mad,
O whistle, and I'll come to ye, my lad.

Aye vow and protest that ye care na for me,
And whiles ye may lightly my beauty a wee;
But court nae anither, tho' jokin' ye be,
For fear that she wile your fancy frae me.
For fear that she wile your fancy frae me.

O whistle, and I'll come to ye, my lad,
O whistle, and I'll come to ye, my lad,
Tho' father and mither and a' should gae mad,
O whistle, and I'll come to ye, my lad.

Comin' Thro' the Rye

Gin a body meet a body
    Comin' thro' the rye,
Gin a body kiss a body,
    Need a body cry?

Every lassie has her laddie—
    Ne'er a ane hae I;
Yet a' the lads they smile at me
    When comin' thro' the rye.

Amang the train there is a swain
    I dearly lo'e mysel';

But whaur his hame, or what his name,
　I dinna care to tell.

Gin a body meet a body
　　Comin' frae the town,
Gin a body greet a body,
　　Need a body frown?

Every lassie has her laddie—
　　Ne'er a ane hae I;
Yet a' the lads they smile at me
　　When comin' thro' the rye.

Amang the train there is a swain
　I dearly lo'e mysel';
But whaur his hame, or what his name,
　I dinna care to tell.

My Wife's a Winsome Wee Thing

She is a winsome wee thing,
She is a handsome wee thing,
She is a lo'esome wee thing,
This dear wee wife o' mine.

I never saw a fairer,
I never lo'ed a dearer,
And neist my heart I'll wear her,
For fear my jewel tine.

She is a winsome wee thing,
She is a handsome wee thing,
She is a lo'esome wee thing,
This dear wife o' mine.

The warld's wrack we share o't,
The warstle and the care o't:
Wi' her I'll blythely bear it,
And think my lot divine.

The Day Returns, My Bosom Burns

The day returns, my bosom burns;
   The blissful day we twa did meet;
Though winter wild in tempest toiled,
   Ne'er summer sun was half sae sweet.
Than a' the pride that loads the tide,
   And crosses o'er the sultry line—
Than kingly robes, and crowns and globes,
   Heaven gave me more; it made thee mine.

While day and night can bring delight,
   Or nature aught of pleasure give—
While joys above my mind can move,
   For thee and thee alone I live;
When that grim foe of life below
   Comes in between to make us part,
The iron hand that breaks our band,
   It breaks my bliss—it breaks my heart.

WILLIAM WORDSWORTH
(1770–1850)

Strange Fits of Passion Have I Known

Strange fits of passion have I known:
 And I will dare to tell,
But in the lover's ear alone,
 What once to me befell.

When she I loved look'd every day
 Fresh as a rose in June,
I to her cottage bent my way,
 Beneath an evening moon.

Upon the moon I fix'd my eye,
 All over the wide lea;
With quickening pace my horse drew nigh
 Those paths so dear to me.

And now we reach'd the orchard-plot;
 And, as we climb'd the hill,
The sinking moon to Lucy's cot
 Came near and nearer still.

In one of those sweet dreams I slept,
 Kind Nature's gentlest boon!
And all the while my eyes I kept
 On the descending moon.

My horse moved on; hoof after hoof
    He raised, and never stopp'd:
When down behind the cottage roof,
    At once, the bright moon dropp'd.

What fond and wayward thoughts will slide
    Into a lover's head!
"O mercy!" to myself I cried,
    "If Lucy should be dead!"

She Dwelt Among the Untrodden Ways

She dwelt among the untrodden ways
    Beside the springs of Dove,
A Maid whom there were none to praise
    And very few to love:

A violet by a mossy stone,
    Half hidden from the eye!
Fair as a star, when only one
    Is shining in the sky.

She lived unknown, and few could know
    When Lucy ceased to be;
But she is in her grave, and oh,
    The difference to me!

I Travell'd Among Unknown Men

I travell'd among unknown men,
    In lands beyond the sea;

Nor, England! did I know till then
    What love I bore to thee.

'Tis past, that melancholy dream!
    Nor will I quit thy shore
A second time; for still I seem
    To love thee more and more.

Among the mountains did I feel
    The joy of my desire;
And she I cherish'd turn'd her wheel
    Beside an English fire.

Thy mornings show'd, thy nights conceal'd,
    The bowers where Lucy play'd;
And thine too is the last green field
    That Lucy's eyes survey'd.

Three Years She Grew in Sun and Shower

Three years she grew in sun and shower;
Then Nature said, "A lovelier flower
    On earth was never sown;
This child I to myself will take;
She shall be mine, and I will make
    A lady of my own.

"Myself will to my darling be
Both law and impulse; and with me
    The girl, in rock and plain,
In earth and heaven, in glade and bower,

Shall feel an overseeing power
  To kindle or restrain.

"She shall be sportive as the fawn
That wild with glee across the lawn
    Or up the mountain springs;
And hers shall be the breathing balm,
And hers the silence and the calm
    Of mute insensate things.

"The floating clouds their state shall lend
To her; for her the willow bend;
    Nor shall she fail to see
Even in the motions of the storm
Grace that shall mould the maiden's form
    By silent sympathy.

"The stars of midnight shall be dear
To her; and she shall lean her ear
    In many a secret place
Where rivulets dance their wayward round,
And beauty born of murmuring sound
    Shall pass into her face.

"And vital feelings of delight
Shall rear her form to stately height,
    Her virgin bosom swell;
Such thoughts to Lucy I will give
While she and I together live
    Here in this happy dell."

Thus Nature spake—the work was done—
How soon my Lucy's race was run!
    She died, and left to me
This heath, this calm and quiet scene;
The memory of what has been,
    And never more will be.

A Slumber Did My Spirit Seal

A slumber did my spirit seal;
    I had no human fears:
She seem'd a thing that could not feel
    The touch of earthly years.

No motion has she now, no force;
    She neither hears nor sees;
Roll'd round in earth's diurnal course,
    With rocks, and stones, and trees.

The World Is Too Much with Us

The world is too much with us: late and soon,
Getting and spending, we lay waste our powers:
Little we see in Nature that is ours;
We have given our hearts away, a sordid boon!
This Sea that bares her bosom to the moon;
The winds that will be howling at all hours,
And are up-gather'd now like sleeping flowers;
For this, for everything, we are out of tune;
It moves us not.—Great God! I'd rather be
A Pagan suckled in a creed outworn;

So might I, standing on this pleasant lea,
Have glimpses that would make me less forlorn;
Have sight of Proteus rising from the sea;
Or hear old Triton blow his wreathèd horn.

Surprised by Joy

Surprised by joy—impatient as the Wind
I turned to share the transport—Oh! with whom
But Thee, long buried in the silent Tomb,
That spot which no vicissitude can find?
Love, faithful love, recalled thee to my mind—
But how could I forget thee?—Through what power,
Even for the least division of an hour,
Have I been so beguiled as to be blind
To my most grievous loss!—That thought's return
Was the worst pang that sorrow ever bore,
Save one, one only, when I stood forlorn,
Knowing my heart's best treasure was no more;
That neither present time, nor years unborn
Could to my sight that heavenly face restore.

She Was a Phantom of Delight

She was a phantom of delight
When first she gleamed upon my sight;
A lovely Apparition, sent
To be a moment's ornament;
Her eyes as stars of twilight fair;
Like Twilight's, too, her dusky hair;
But all things else about her drawn

From May-time and the cheerful dawn;
A dancing shape, an image gay,
To haunt, to startle, and waylay.

I saw her upon nearer view,
A Spirit, yet a Woman too!
Her household motions light and free,
And steps of virgin-liberty;
A countenance in which did meet
Sweet records, promises as sweet;
A creature not too bright or good
For human nature's daily food,
For transient sorrows, simple wiles,
Praise, blame, love, kisses, tears, and smiles.

And now I see with eye serene
The very pulse of the machine;
A being breathing thoughtful breath,
A traveller between life and death:
The reason firm, the temperate will,
Endurance, foresight, strength, and skill;
A perfect Woman, nobly planned
To warn, to comfort, and command;
And yet a Spirit still, and bright
With something of an angel-light.

SIR WALTER SCOTT
(1771–1832)

Love

From THE LAY OF THE LAST MINSTREL

And said I that my limbs were old,
And said I that my blood was cold,
And that my kindly fire was fled,
And my poor withered heart was dead,
   And that I might not sing of love?—
How could I, to the dearest theme
That ever warmed a minstrel's dream,
   So foul, so false a recreant prove!
How could I name love's very name,
Nor wake my heart to notes of flame!

* * * * *

In peace, Love tunes the shepherd's reed;
In war, he mounts the warrior's steed;
In halls, in gay attire is seen;
In hamlets, dances on the green.
Love rules the court, the camp, the grove,
And men below, and saints above;
For love is heaven, and heaven is love.

Lochinvar

From MARMION

O, young Lochinvar is come out of the west,
Through all the wide Border his steed was the best;
And save his good broadsword he weapon had none,
He rode all unarm'd, and he rode all alone.
So faithful in love, and so dauntless in war,
There never was knight like the young Lochinvar.

He staid not for brake, and he stopp'd not for stone,
He swam the Eske River where ford there was none;
But ere he alighted at Netherby gate,
The bride had consented, the gallant came late;
For a laggard in love, and a dastard in war,
Was to wed the fair Ellen of brave Lochinvar.

So boldly he enter'd the Netherby Hall,
Among bridesmen, and kinsmen, and brothers, and all.
Then spoke the bride's father, his hand on his sword
  (For the poor craven bridegroom said never a word),
"O, come ye in peace here, or come ye in war,
  Or to dance at our bridal, young Lord Lochinvar?"

"I long wooed your daughter, my suit you denied;—
Love swells like the Solway, but ebbs like its tide,—
And now I am come, with this lost love of mine,
To lead but one measure, drink one cup of wine.
There are maidens in Scotland more lovely by far,
That would gladly be bride to the young Lochinvar."

The bride kissed the goblet; the knight took it up,
He quaffed off the wine, and threw down the cup.
She looked down to blush, and she looked up to sigh,
With a smile on her lips, and a tear in her eye.
He took her soft hand, ere her mother could bar,—
"Now tread we a measure!" said young Lochinvar.

So stately his form, and so lovely her face,
That never a hall such a galliard did grace;
While her mother did fret, and her father did fume,
And the bridegroom stood dangling his bonnet and plume;
And the bridemaidens whispered, "'T were better by far
To have matched our fair cousin with young Lochinvar."

One touch to her hand, and one word in her ear,
When they reached the hall-door, and the charger stood
        near;
So light to the croupe the fair lady he swung,
So light to the saddle before her he sprung;
"She is won! we are gone! over bank, bush, and scaur;
They 'll have fleet steeds that follow," quoth young
        Lochinvar.

There was mounting 'mong Græmes of the Netherby clan;
Forsters, Fenwicks, and Musgraves, they rode and they ran;
There was racing and chasing on Cannobie Lee,
But the lost bride of Netherby ne'er did they see.
So daring in love, and so dauntless in war,
Have ye e'er heard of gallant like young Lochinvar?

SAMUEL TAYLOR COLERIDGE
(1772–1834)

Love

All thoughts, all passions, all delights,
Whatever stirs this mortal frame,
All are but ministers of Love,
    And feed his sacred flame.

Oft in my waking dreams do I
Live o'er again that happy hour,
When midway on the mount I lay,
    Beside the ruined tower.

The moonshine, stealing o'er the scene
Had blended with the lights of eve;
And she was there, my hope, my joy,
    My own dear Genevieve!

She leant against the armèd man,
The statue of the armèd knight;
She stood and listened to my lay,
    Amid the lingering light.

Few sorrows hath she of her own,
My hope! my joy! my Genevieve!
She loves me best, whene'er I sing
    The songs that make her grieve.

I play'd a soft and doleful air,
I sang an old and moving story—
An old rude song, that suited well
    That ruin wild and hoary.

She listened with a flitting blush,
With downcast eyes and modest grace;
For well she knew, I could not choose
    But gaze upon her face.

I told her of the Knight that wore
Upon his shield a burning brand;
And that for ten long years he woo'd
    The Lady of the Land.

I told her how he pined: and ah!
The deep, the low, the pleading tone
With which I sang another's love,
    Interpreted my own.

She listened with a flitting blush,
With downcast eyes, and modest grace;
And she forgave me, that I gazed
    Too fondly on her face!

But when I told the cruel scorn
That crazed that bold and lovely Knight,
And that he cross'd the mountain-woods,
    Nor rested day nor night;

That sometimes from the savage den,
And sometimes from the darksome shade,
And sometimes starting up at once
  In green and sunny glade—

There came and look'd him in the face
An angel beautiful and bright;
And that he knew it was a Fiend,
  This miserable Knight!

And that, unknowing what he did,
He leaped amid a murderous band,
And saved from outrage worse than death
  The Lady of the Land!

And how she wept, and clasp'd his knees;
And how she tended him in vain—
And ever strove to expiate
  The scorn that crazed his brain—

And that she nursed him in a cave;
And how his madness went away,
When on the yellow forest-leaves
  A dying man he lay—

His dying words—but when I reached
That tenderest strain of all the ditty,
My faltering voice and pausing harp
  Disturb'd her soul with pity!

All impulses of soul and sense
Had thrill'd my guileless Genevieve;
The music and the doleful tale,
      The rich and balmy eve;

And hopes, and fears that kindle hope,
An undistinguishable throng,
And gentle wishes long subdued,
      Subdued and cherish'd long!

She wept with pity and delight,
She blushed with love, and virgin-shame;
And like the murmur of a dream,
      I heard her breathe my name.

Her bosom heaved—she stepp'd aside,
As conscious of my look she stepp'd—
Then suddenly, with timorous eye
      She fled to me and wept.

She half enclosed me with her arms,
She press'd me with a meek embrace;
And bending back her head, looked up,
      And gazed upon my face.

'Twas partly love, and partly fear,
And partly 'twas a bashful art,
That I might rather feel, than see,
      The swelling of her heart.

I calmed her fears, and she was calm,
And told her love with virgin pride;
And so I won my Genevieve,
  My bright and beauteous Bride.

The Presence of Love

And in Life's noisiest hour,
There whispers still the ceaseless Love of Thee,
The heart's Self-solace and soliloquy.
You mould my Hopes, you fashion me within;
And to the leading Love-throb in the Heart
Thro' all my Being, thro' my pulse's beat;
You lie in all my many Thoughts, like Light,
Like the fair light of Dawn, or summer Eve
On rippling Stream, or cloud-reflecting Lake;
And looking to the Heaven, that bends above you,
How oft! I bless the Lot that made me love you.

The Exchange

We pledged our hearts, my love and I—
  I in my arms the maiden clasping;
I could not tell the reason why,
  But, O, I trembled like an aspen!

Her father's love she bade me gain;
  I went, and shook like any reed!
I strove to act the man—in vain!
  We had exchanged our hearts indeed.

To Two Sisters

[MARY MORGAN AND CHARLOTTE BRENT]

A WANDERER'S FAREWELL

To know, to esteem, to love—and then to part—
Makes up life's tale to many a feeling heart;
Alas for some abiding-place of love,
O'er which my spirit, like the mother dove,
Might brood with warming wings!

                                 O fair! O kind!

Sisters in blood, yet each with each intwined
More close by sisterhood of heart and mind!
Me disinherited in form and face
By nature, and mishap of outward grace;
Who, soul and body, through one guiltless fault
Waste daily with the poison of sad thought,
Me did you soothe, when solace hoped I none!
And as on unthaw'd ice the winter sun,
Though stern the frost, though brief the genial day,
You bless my heart with many a cheerful ray;
For gratitude suspends the heart's despair,
Reflecting bright though cold your image there.
Nay more! its music by some sweeter strain
Makes us live o'er our happiest hours again,
Hope re-appearing dim in memory's guise—
Even thus did you call up before mine eyes
Two dear, dear Sisters, prized all price above,
Sisters, like you, with more than sisters' love;
So like you *they*, and so in *you* were seen

Their relative statures, tempers, looks, and mien,
That oft, dear ladies! you have been to me
At once a vision and reality.
Sight seem'd a sort of memory, and amaze
Mingled a trouble with affection's gaze.

Oft to my eager soul I whisper blame,
A Stranger bid it feel the Stranger's shame—
My eager soul, impatient of the name,
No strangeness owns, no Stranger's form descries:
The chidden heart spreads trembling on the eyes.
First-seen I gazed, as I would look you thro'!
My best-beloved regain'd their youth in you—
And still I ask, though now familiar grown,
Are you for *their* sakes dear, or for your own?
O doubly dear! may Quiet with you dwell!
In Grief I love you, yet I love you well!
Hope long is dead to me! an orphan's tear
Love wept despairing o'er his nurse's bier.
Yet still she flutters o'er her grave's green slope:
For Love's despair is but the ghost of Hope!
Sweet Sisters! were you placed around one hearth
With those, your other selves in shape and worth,
Far rather would I sit in solitude,
Fond recollections all my fond heart's food,
And dream of *you*, sweet Sisters! (ah! not mine!)
And only *dream* of you (ah! dream and pine!)
Than boast the presence and partake the pride,
And shine in the eye, of all the world beside.

First Advent of Love

O fair is Love's first hope to gentle mind!
As Eve's first star thro' fleecy cloudlet peeping;
And sweeter than the gentle south-west wind,
O'er willowy meads and shadowed waters creeping,
And Ceres' golden fields—the sultry hind
Meets it with brow uplift, and stays his reaping.

THOMAS CAMPBELL
(1777–1844)

The First Kiss

How delicious is the winning
Of a kiss at love's beginning,
When two mutual hearts are sighing
For the knot there's no untying!

Yet remember, midst your wooing,
Love has bliss, but love has ruing;
Other smiles may make you fickle,
Tears for other charms may trickle.

Love he comes, Love he tarries,
Just as fate or fancy carries—
Longest stays when sorest chidden,
Laughs and flies when pressed and bidden.

Bind the sea to slumber stilly,
Bind its odor to the lily,
Bind the aspen ne'er to quiver—
Then bind Love to last forever!

Love's a fire that needs renewal
Of fresh beauty for its fuel;
Love's wing moults when caged and captured—
Only free he soars enraptured.

Can you keep the bee from ranging,
Or the ring-dove's neck from changing?
No! nor fettered Love from dying
In the knot there's no untying.

To the Evening Star

Star that bringest home the bee,
And sett'st the weary labourer free!
If any star shed peace, 'tis thou,
That send'st it from above,
Appearing when Heaven's breath and brow
Are sweet as hers we love.

Come to the luxuriant skies,
Whilst the landscape's odours rise,
Whilst far-off lowing herds are heard,
And songs when toil is done,
From cottages whose smoke unstirr'd
Curls yellow in the sun.

Star of love's soft interviews.
Parted lovers on thee muse;
Their remembrancer in heaven
Of thrilling vows thou art,
Too delicious to be riven
By absence from the heart.

THOMAS MOORE
(1779–1852)

Echoes

How sweet the answer Echo makes
To Music at night
When, roused by lute or horn, she wakes,
And far away o'er lawns and lakes
Goes answering light!

Yet Love hath echoes truer far
And far more sweet
Than e'er, beneath the moonlight's star,
Of horn or lute or soft guitar
The songs repeat.

'T is when the sigh—in youth sincere
And only then,
The sigh that's breathed for one to hear—
Is by that one, that only Dear,
Breathed back again.

Love's Young Dream

O the days are gone when Beauty bright
    My heart's chain wove!
When my dream of life, from morn till night,
    Was love, still love!
    New hope may bloom,
    And days may come,

Of milder, calmer beam,
But there's nothing half so sweet in life
As love's young dream!
No, there's nothing half so sweet in life
As love's young dream!

Tho' the bard to purer fame may soar,
When wild youth's past;
Tho' he win the wise, who frown'd before,
To smile at last;
He'll never meet
A joy so sweet
In all his noon of fame
As when first he sung to woman's ear
His soul-felt flame,
And at every close she blush'd to hear
The one loved name!

No—that hallowed form is ne'er forgot,
Which first love traced;
Still it lingering haunts the greenest spot
On memory's waste.
'Twas odor fled
As soon as shed;
'Twas morning's wingèd dream;
'Twas a light that ne'er can shine again
On life's dull stream:
O, 'twas a light that ne'er can shine again
On life's dull stream.

LEIGH HUNT
(1784–1859)

Jenny Kiss'd Me

Jenny kiss'd me when we met,
    Jumping from the chair she sat in;
Time, you thief, who love to get
    Sweets into your list, put that in!
Say I'm weary, say I'm sad,
    Say that health and wealth have miss'd me,
Say I'm growing old, but add,
    Jenny kiss'd me.

GEORGE GORDON, LORD BYRON
(1788–1824)

She Walks in Beauty

She walks in beauty, like the night
Of cloudless climes and starry skies;
And all that's best of dark and bright
Meet in her aspect and her eyes;
Thus mellow'd to that tender light
Which heaven to gaudy day denies.

One shade the more, one ray the less,
Had half impair'd the nameless grace
Which waves in every raven tress,
Or softly lightens o'er her face;
Where thoughts serenely sweet express
How pure, how dear their dwelling-place.

And on that cheek, and o'er that brow,
So soft, so calm, yet eloquent,
The smiles that win, the tints that glow;
But tell of days in goodness spent,
A mind at peace with all below,
A heart whose love is innocent!

There Be None of Beauty's Daughters

There be none of Beauty's daughters
With a magic like thee;
And like music on the waters
Is thy sweet voice to me:
When, as if its sound were causing
The charmed ocean's pausing,
The waves lie still and gleaming,
And the lull'd winds seem dreaming:

And the midnight moon is weaving
Her bright chain o'er the deep,
Whose breast is gently heaving
As an infant's asleep:
So the spirit bows before thee
To listen and adore thee;
With a full but soft emotion,
Like the swell of Summer's ocean.

When We Two Parted

When we two parted
In silence and tears,
Half broken-hearted
To sever for years,
Pale grew thy cheek and cold,
Colder thy kiss;
Truly that hour foretold
Sorrow to this.

The dew of the morning
Sunk chill on my brow—
It felt like the warning
Of what I feel now.
Thy vows are all broken,
And light is thy fame:
I hear thy name spoken,
And share in its shame.

They name thee before me,
A knell to mine ear;
A shudder comes o'er me—
Why wert thou so dear?
They know not I knew thee,
Who knew thee too well:
Long, long shall I rue thee,
Too deeply to tell.

In secret we met—
In silence I grieve,
That thy heart could forget,
Thy spirit deceive.
If I should meet thee
After long years,
How should I greet thee?
With silence and tears.

We'll Go No More a-Roving

So, we'll go no more a-roving
So late into the night,
Though the heart be still as loving,
And the moon be still as bright.

For the sword outwears its sheath,
And the soul wears out the breast,
And the heart must pause to breathe,
And love itself have rest.

Though the night was made for loving,
And the day returns too soon,
Yet we'll go no more a-roving
By the light of the moon.

All for Love

O talk not to me of a name great in story;
The days of our youth are the days of our glory;
And the myrtle and ivy of sweet two-and-twenty
Are worth all your laurels though ever so plenty.

What are garlands and crowns to the brow that is wrinkled?
'Tis but as a dead flower with May-dew besprinkled:
Then away with all such from the head that is hoary—
What care I for the wreaths that can only give glory?

O Fame! if I e'er took delight in thy praises,
'Twas less for the sake of thy high-sounding phrases,

Than to see the bright eyes of the dear one discover
She thought that I was not unworthy to love her.

There chiefly I sought thee, there only I found thee;
Her glance was the best of the rays that surround thee;
When it sparkled o'er aught that was bright in my story
I knew it was love and I felt it was glory.

Remind Me Not, Remind Me Not

Remind me not, remind me not,
Of those beloved, those vanish'd hours,
When all my soul was given to thee;
Hours that may never be forgot,
Till Time unnerves our vital powers,
And thou and I shall cease to be.

Can I forget—canst thou forget,
When playing with thy golden hair,
How quick thy fluttering heart did move?
Oh! by my soul, I see thee yet,
With eyes so languid, breast so fair,
And lips, though silent, breathing love.

When thus reclining on my breast,
Those eyes threw back a glance so sweet,
As half reproach'd yet rais'd desire,
And still we near and nearer prest,
And still our glowing lips would meet,
As if in kisses to expire.

And then those pensive eyes would close,
And bid their lids each other seek,
Veiling the azure orbs below;
While their long lashes' darken'd gloss
Seem'd stealing o'er thy brilliant cheek,
Like raven's plumage smooth'd on snow.

I dreamt last night our love return'd,
And, sooth to say, that very dream
Was sweeter in its phantasy,
Than if for other hearts I burn'd,
For eyes that ne'er like thine could beam
In Rapture's wild reality.

Then tell me not, remind me not,
Of hours which, though for ever gone,
Can still a pleasing dream restore,
Till Thou and I shall be forgot,
And senseless, as the mouldering stone
Which tells that we shall be no more.

And Wilt Thou Weep When I Am Low?

And wilt thou weep when I am low?
Sweet lady! speak those words again:
Yet if they grieve thee, say not so—
I would not give that bosom pain.

My heart is sad, my hopes are gone,
My blood runs coldly through my breast;

And when I perish, thou alone
Wilt sigh above my place of rest.

And yet, methinks, a gleam of peace
Doth through my cloud of anguish shine:
And for a while my sorrows cease,
To know thy heart hath felt for mine.

Oh lady! blessèd be that tear—
It falls for one who cannot weep;
Such precious drops are doubly dear
To those whose eyes no tear may steep.

Sweet lady! once my heart was warm
With every feeling soft as thine;
But Beauty's self hath ceased to charm
A wretch created to repine.

Yet wilt thou weep when I am low?
Sweet lady! speak those words again:
Yet if they grieve thee, say not so—
I would not give that bosom pain.

I Speak Not

I speak not, I trace not, I breathe not thy name;
There is grief in the sound, there is guilt in the fame;
But the tear that now burns on my cheek may impart
The deep thoughts that dwell in that silence of heart.

Too brief for our passion, too long for our peace,
Were those hours—can their joy or their bitterness cease?
We repent, we abjure, we will break from our chain—
We will part, we will fly—to unite it again!

Oh! thine be the gladness, and mine be the guilt!
Forgive me, adored one!—forsake, if thou wilt;
But the heart which is thine shall expire undebased,
And *man* shall not break it—whatever *thou* may'st.

And stern to the haughty, but humble to thee,
This soul, in its bitterest blackness, shall be;
And our days seem as swift, and our moments more
    sweet,
With thee at my side, than with worlds at our feet.

One sigh of thy sorrow, one look of thy love,
Shall turn me or fix, shall reward or reprove;
And the heartless may wonder at all I resign—
Thy lips shall reply, not to them, but to *mine*.

Sonnet to Genevra

Thy cheek is pale with thought, but not from woe,
And yet so lovely, that if Mirth could flush
Its rose of whiteness with the brightest blush,
My heart would wish away that ruder glow:
And dazzle not thy deep-blue eyes—but, oh!
While gazing on them sterner eyes will gush,
And into mine my mother's weakness rush,
Soft as the last drops round Heaven's airy bow.

For, though thy long dark lashes low depending,
The soul of melancholy Gentleness
Gleams like a Seraph from the sky descending,
Above all pain, yet pitying all distress;
At once such majesty with sweetness blending,
I worship more, but cannot love thee less.

Maid of Athens, Ere We Part

Zoë mou, sas agapo. [My life, I love you.]

Maid of Athens, ere we part,
Give, oh, give back my heart!
Or, since that has left my breast,
Keep it now, and take the rest!
Hear my vow before I go,
Zoë mou, sas agapo.

By those tresses unconfined,
Woo'd by each Aegean wind;
By those lids whose jetty fringe
Kiss thy soft cheeks' blooming tinge;
By those wild eyes like the roe,
Zoë mou, sas agapo.

By that lip I long to taste;
By that zone-encircled waist;
By all the token-flowers that tell
What words can never speak so well;
By love's alternate joy and woe,
Zoë mou, sas agapo.

Maid of Athens! I am gone:
Think of me, sweet! when alone.
Though I fly to Istambol,
Athens holds my heart and soul:
Can I cease to love thee? No!
Zoë mou, sas agapo.

To Caroline

Think'st thou I saw thy beauteous eyes,
Suffus'd in tears, implore to stay;
And heard unmov'd thy plenteous sighs,
Which said far more than words can say?

Though keen the grief thy tears exprest,
When love and hope lay both o'erthrown;
Yet still, my girl, this bleeding breast
Throbb'd, with deep sorrow, as thine own.

But, when our cheeks with anguish glow'd,
When thy sweet lips were join'd to mine;
The tears that from my eyelids flow'd
Were lost in those which fell from thine.

Thou could'st not feel my burning cheek,
Thy gushing tears had quench'd its flame,
And, as thy tongue essay'd to speak,
In sighs alone it breath'd my name.

And yet, my girl, we weep in vain,
In vain our fate in sighs deplore;

Remembrance only can remain,
But that, will make us weep the more.

Again, thou best belov'd, adieu!
Ah! if thou canst, o'ercome regret,
Nor let thy mind past joys review,
Our only hope is, to forget!

PERCY BYSSHE SHELLEY
(1792–1822)

The Indian Serenade

I arise from dreams of thee
In the first sweet sleep of night,
When the winds are breathing low,
And the stars are shining bright.
I arise from dreams of thee,
And a spirit in my feet
Hath led me—who knows how?
To thy chamber window, Sweet!

The wandering airs they faint
On the dark, the silent stream—
And the Champak's odours pine
Like sweet thoughts in a dream;
The nightingale's complaint,
It dies upon her heart,
As I must on thine,
O beloved as thou art!

O lift me from the grass!
I die! I faint! I fail!
Let thy love in kisses rain
On my lips and eyelids pale.
My cheek is cold and white, alas!
My heart beats loud and fast:
O press it to thine own again,
Where it will break at last!

Song

Rarely, rarely, comest thou,
    Spirit of Delight!
Wherefore hast thou left me now
    Many a day and night?
Many a weary night and day
'Tis since thou art fled away.

How shall ever one like me
    Win thee back again?
With the joyous and the free
    Thou wilt scoff at pain.
Spirit false! thou hast forgot
All but those who need thee not.

As a lizard with the shade
    Of a trembling leaf,
Thou with sorrow art dismay'd;
    Even the sighs of grief
Reproach thee, that thou art not near,
And reproach thou wilt not hear.

Let me set my mournful ditty
    To a merry measure;
Thou wilt never come for pity,
    Thou wilt come for pleasure;
Pity then will cut away
Those cruel wings, and thou wilt stay.

I love all that thou lovest,
    Spirit of Delight!
The fresh Earth in new leaves dress'd,
    And the starry night;
Autumn evening, and the morn
When the golden mists are born.

I love snow, and all the forms
    Of the radiant frost;
I love waves, and winds, and storms,
    Everything almost
Which is Nature's, and may be
Untainted by man's misery.

I love tranquil solitude,
    And such society
As is quiet, wise, and good;
    Between thee and me
What difference? but thou dost possess
The things I seek, not love them less.

I love Love—though he has wings,
    And like light can flee,
But above all other things,
    Spirit, I love thee—
Thou art love and life! O, come,
Make once more my heart thy home.

To Jane: The Invitation

Best and brightest, come away!
Fairer far than this fair Day,
Which, like thee to those in sorrow,
Comes to bid a sweet good-morrow
To the rough Year just awake
In its cradle on the brake.
The Brightest hour of unborn Spring,
Through the winter wandering,
Found, it seems, the halcyon Morn
To hoar February born.
Bending from Heaven, in azure mirth,
It kissed the forehead of the Earth,
And smiled upon the silent sea,
And bade the frozen streams be free,
And waked to music all their fountains,
And breathed upon the frozen mountains,
And like a prophetess of May
Strewed flowers upon the barren way,
Making the wintry world appear
Like one on whom thou smilest, dear.
Away, away, from men and towns,
To the wild wood and the downs—
To the silent wilderness
Where the soul need not repress
Its music lest it should not find
An echo in another's mind.
While the touch of Nature's art
Harmonizes heart to heart.
I leave this notice on my door

For each accustomed visitor—
"I am gone into the fields
To take what this sweet hour yields—
Reflection, you may come tomorrow,
Sit by the fireside with Sorrow.
You with the unpaid bill, Despair—
You, tiresome verse-reciter, Care—
I will pay you in the grave—
Death will listen to your stave.
Expectation too, be off!
To-day is for itself enough;
Hope, in pity mock not Woe
With smiles, nor follow where I go;
Long having lived on thy sweet food,
At length I find one moment's good
After long pain—with all your love,
This you never told me of."

Radiant Sister of the Day,
Awake! arise! And come away!
To the wild woods and the plains,
And the pools where winter rains
Image all their roof of leaves,
Where the pine its garland weaves
Of sapless green, and ivy dun
Round stems that never kiss the sun:
Where the lawns and pastures be,
And the sandhills of the sea—
Where the melting hoar-frost wets
The daisy-star that never sets,
And wind-flowers, and violets,

Which yet join not scent to hue,
Crown the pale year weak and new;
When the night is left behind
In the deep east, dun and blind,
And the blue noon is over us,
And the multitudinous
Billows murmur at our feet,
Where the earth and ocean meet,
And all things seem only one
In the universal sun.

One Word Is Too Often Profaned

One word is too often profaned
For me to profane it;
One feeling too falsely disdained
For thee to disdain it;
One hope is too like despair
For prudence to smother;
And pity from thee more dear
Than that from another.

I can give not what men call love;
But wilt thou accept not
The worship the heart lifts above
And the heavens reject not—
The desire of the moth for the star,
Of the night for the morrow,
The devotion to something afar
From the sphere of our sorrow?

Love's Philosophy

The fountains mingle with the river
   And the rivers with the ocean,
The winds of heaven mix for ever
   With a sweet emotion;
Nothing in the world is single;
   All things by a law divine
In one spirit meet and mingle.
   Why not I with thine?—

See the mountains kiss high heaven
   And the waves clasp one another;
No sister-flower would be forgiven
   If it disdained its brother;
And the sunlight clasps the earth
   And the moonbeams kiss the sea:
What is all this sweet work worth
   If thou kiss not me?

When the Lamp Is Shattered

When the lamp is shattered
The light in the dust lies dead—
   When the cloud is scattered
The rainbow's glory is shed.
   When the lute is broken,
Sweet tones are remembered not;
   When the lips have spoken,
Loved accents are soon forgot.

As music and splendour
Survive not the lamp and the lute,
The heart's echoes render
No song when the spirit is mute—
No song but sad dirges,
Like the wind through a ruined cell,
Or the mournful surges
That ring the dead seaman's knell.

When hearts have once mingled
Love first leaves the well-built nest;
The weak one is singled
To endure what it once possessed.
O Love! who bewailest
The frailty of all things here,
Why choose you the frailest
For your cradle, your home, and your bier?

Its passions will rock thee
As the storms rock the ravens on high;
Bright reason will mock thee,
Like the sun from a wintry sky.
From thy nest every rafter
Will rot, and thine eagle home
Leave thee naked to laughter,
When leaves fall and cold winds come.

JOHN KEATS

(1795–1821)

A Thing of Beauty

From ENDYMION

A thing of beauty is a joy for ever:
Its loveliness increases; it will never
Pass into nothingness; but still will keep
A bower quiet for us, and a sleep
Full of sweet dreams, and health, and quiet breathing.
Therefore, on every morrow, are we wreathing
A flowery band to bind us to the earth,
Spite of despondence, of the inhuman dearth
Of noble natures, of the gloomy days,
Of all the unhealthy and o'er-darkened ways
Made for our searching: yes, in spite of all,
Some shape of beauty moves away the pall
From our dark spirits. Such the sun, the moon,
Trees old and young, sprouting a shady boon
For simple sheep; and such are daffodils
With the green world they live in; and clear rills
That for themselves a cooling covert make
'Gainst the hot season; the mid-forest brake,
Rich with a sprinkling of fair musk-rose blooms:
And such too is the grandeur of the dooms
We have imagined for the mighty dead;
All lovely tales that we have heard or read:
An endless fountain of immortal drink,
Pouring unto us from the heaven's brink.

Ode to Fanny

Physician Nature! Let my spirit blood!
    O ease my heart of verse and let me rest;
Throw me upon thy Tripod, till the flood
    Of stifling numbers ebbs from my full breast.
A theme! a theme! great nature! give a theme;
      Let me begin my dream.
I come—I see thee, as thou standest there,
Beckon me not into the wintry air.

Ah! dearest love, sweet home of all my fears,
    And hopes, and joys, and panting miseries—
Tonight, if I may guess, thy beauty wears
      A smile of such delight,
      As brilliant and as bright,
    As when with ravished, aching, vassal eyes,
      Lost in soft amaze,
      I gaze, I gaze!

Who now, with greedy looks, eats up my feast?
    What stare outfaces now my silver moon!
Ah! keep that hand unravished at the least;
      Let, let, the amorous burn—
      But pr'ythee, do not turn
The current of your heart from me so soon.
      O! save, in charity,
      The quickest pulse for me.

Save it for me, sweet love! though music breathe
    Voluptuous visions into the warm air;
Though swimming through the dance's dangerous wreath,
       Be like an April day,
       Smiling and cold and gay,
    A temperate lilly, temperate as fair;
       Then, Heaven! there will be
       A warmer June for me.

Why, this, you'll say, my Fanny! is not true:
    Put your soft hand upon your snowy side,
Where the heart beats: confess—'tis nothing new—
       Must not a woman be
       A feather on the sea,
    Sway'd to and fro by every wind and tide?
       Of as uncertain speed
       As blow-ball from the mead?

I know it—and to know it is despair
    To one who loves you as I love, sweet Fanny!
Whose heart goes fluttering for you every where,
       Nor, when away you roam,
       Dare keep its wretched home,
    Love, love alone, his pains severe and many:
       Then, loveliest! keep me free,
       From torturing jealousy.

Ah! if you prize my subdued soul above
    The poor, the fading, brief, pride of an hour;
Let none profane my Holy See of love,
       Or with a rude hand break
       The sacramental cake:
    Let none else touch the just new-budded flower;
       If not—may my eyes close,
       Love! on their lost repose.

Bright Star, Would I Were Steadfast

Bright star, would I were steadfast as thou art—
    Not in lone splendour hung aloft the night
And watching, with eternal lids apart,
    Like nature's patient, sleepless Eremite,
The moving waters at their priestlike task
    Of pure ablution round earth's human shores,
Or gazing on the new soft-fallen mask
    Of snow upon the mountains and the moors—
No—yet still steadfast, still unchangeable,
    Pillow'd upon my fair love's ripening breast,
To feel for ever its soft fall and swell,
    Awake for ever in a sweet unrest,
Still, still to hear her tender-taken breath,
And so live ever—or else swoon to death.

Charles Swain
(1801–1874)

A Violet in Her Hair

A violet in her lovely hair,
A rose upon her bosom fair!
 But O, her eyes
A lovelier violet disclose,
And her ripe lips the sweetest rose
 That's 'neath the skies.

A lute beneath her graceful hand
Breathes music forth at her command;
 But still her tongue
Far richer music calls to birth
Than all the minstrel power on earth
 Can give to song.

And thus she moves in tender light,
The purest ray, where all is bright,
 Serene, and sweet;
And sheds a graceful influence round,
That hallows e'en the very ground
 Beneath her feet!

ELIZABETH BARRETT BROWNING
(1806–1861)

Sonnet 6

Go from me. Yet I feel that I shall stand
Henceforward in thy shadow. Nevermore
Alone upon the threshold of my door
Of individual life, I shall command
The uses of my soul, nor lift my hand
Serenely in the sunshine as before,
Without the sense of that which I forbore . . .
Thy touch upon the palm. The widest land
Doom takes to part us, leaves thy heart in mine
With pulses that beat double. What I do
And what I dream include thee, as the wine
Must taste of its own grapes. And when I sue
God for myself, he hears that name of thine,
And sees within my eyes the tears of two.

Sonnet 14

If thou must love me, let it be for nought
Except for love's sake only. Do not say
"I love her for her smile—her look—her way
Of speaking gently—for a trick of thought
That falls in well with mine, and certes brought
A sense of pleasant ease on such a day"—
For these things in themselves, Belovèd, may
Be changed, or change for thee—and love, so wrought,
May be unwrought so. Neither love me for

Thine own dear pity's wiping my cheeks dry—
A creature might forget to weep, who bore
Thy comfort long, and lose thy love thereby!
But love me for love's sake, that evermore
Thou may'st love on, through love's eternity.

Sonnet 18

I never gave a lock of hair away
To a man, Dearest, except this to thee,
Which now upon my fingers thoughtfully
I ring out to the full brown length and say
"Take it." My day of youth went yesterday;
My hair no longer bounds to my foot's glee.
Nor plant I it from rose or myrtle tree,
As girls do, any more. It only may
Now shade on two pale cheeks, the mark of tears,
Taught drooping from the head that hangs aside
Through sorrow's trick. I thought the funeral shears
Would take this first, but Love is justified—
Take it thou . . . finding pure, from all those years,
The kiss my mother left here when she died.

Sonnet 21

Say over again, and yet once over again,
That thou dost love me. Though the word repeated
Should seem a "cuckoo-song," as thou dost treat it,
Remember never to the hill or plain,
Valley and wood, without her cuckoo-strain,
Comes the fresh spring in all her green completed.

Beloved, I, amid the darkness greeted
By a doubtful spirit-voice, in that doubt's pain
Cry: "Speak once more—thou lovest!" Who can fear
Too many stars, though each in heaven shall roll,—
Too many flowers, though each shall crown the year?
Say thou dost love me, love me, love me,—toll
The silver iterance!—only minding, Dear,
To love me also in silence, with thy soul.

Sonnet 35

If I leave all for thee, wilt thou exchange
And be all to me? Shall I never miss
Home-talk and blessing and the common kiss
That comes to each in turn, nor count it strange,
When I look up, to drop on a new range
Of walls and floors, another home than this?
Nay, wilt thou fill that place by me which is
Filled by dead eyes too tender to know change
That 's hardest? If to conquer love, has tried,
To conquer grief, tries more, as all things prove,
For grief indeed is love and grief beside.
Alas, I have grieved so I am hard to love.
Yet love me—wilt thou? Open thine heart wide,
And fold within the wet wings of thy dove.

Sonnet 38

First time he kissed me, he but only kissed
The fingers of this hand wherewith I write;
And, ever since, it grew more clean and white,

Slow to world-greetings, quick with its "O list!"
When the angels speak. A ring of amethyst
I could not wear here, plainer to my sight
Than that first kiss. The second passed in height
The first, and sought the forehead, and half missed,
Half falling on the hair. O, beyond meed!
That was the chrism of love, which love's own crown,
With sanctifying sweetness, did precede.
The third upon my lips was folded down
In perfect, purple state; since when, indeed,
I have been proud, and said, "My love, my own!"

Sonnet 39

Because thou hast the power and own'st the grace
To look through and behind this mask of me,
(Against which, years have beat thus blanchingly
With their rains,) and behold my soul's true face,
The dim and weary witness of life's race—
Because thou hast the faith and love to see,
Through that same soul's distracting lethargy,
The patient angel waiting for a place
In the new Heavens,—because nor sin nor woe,
Nor God's infliction, nor death's neighborhood,
Nor all which others viewing, turn to go,
Nor all which makes me tired of all, self-viewed—
Nothing repels thee . . . Dearest, teach me so
To pour out gratitude, as thou dost, good!

Sonnet 43

How do I love thee? Let me count the ways.
I love thee to the depth and breadth and height
My soul can reach, when feeling out of sight
For the ends of being and ideal grace.
I love thee to the level of every day's
Most quiet need, by sun and candlelight.
I love thee freely, as men strive for right;
I love thee purely, as they turn from praise.
I love thee with the passion put to use
In my old griefs, and with my childhood's faith.
I love thee with a love I seemed to lose
With my lost saints. I love thee with the breath,
Smiles, tears, of all my life; and, if God choose,
I shall but love thee better after death.

EDGAR ALLAN POE
(1809–1849)

Annabel Lee

It was many and many a year ago,
 In a kingdom by the sea,
That a maiden lived whom you may know
 By the name of Annabel Lee;
And this maiden she lived with no other thought
 Than to love and be loved by me.

I was a child and *she* was a child,
 In this kingdom by the sea,
But we loved with a love that was more than love—
 I and my Annabel Lee—
With a love that the wingèd seraphs of Heaven
 Coveted her and me.

And this was the reason that, long ago,
 In this kingdom by the sea,
A wind blew out of a cloud by night
 Chilling my Annabel Lee;
So that her high-born kinsmen came
 And bore her away from me,
To shut her up, in a sepulchre
 In this kingdom by the sea.

The angels, not half so happy in Heaven,
 Went envying her and me;
Yes!—that was the reason (as all men know,

In this kingdom by the sea)
That the wind came out of the cloud, chilling
    And killing my Annabel Lee.

But our love it was stronger by far than the love
    Of those who were older than we—
Of many far wiser than we—
    And neither the angels in Heaven above
Nor the demons down under the sea
    Can ever dissever my soul from the soul
Of the beautiful Annabel Lee,

For the moon never beams without bringing me dreams
    Of the beautiful Annabel Lee;
And the stars never rise but I see the bright eyes
    Of the beautiful Annabel Lee;
And so, all the night-tide, I lie down by the side
    Of my darling—my darling—my life and my bride
In her sepulchre there by the sea—
    In her tomb by the sounding sea.

Eulalie

I dwelt alone
In a world of moan,
And my soul was a stagnant tide,
Till the fair and gentle Eulalie became my blushing bride—
Till the yellow-haired young Eulalie became my smiling bride.

Ah, less—less bright
The stars of the night

Than the eyes of the radiant girl!
    And never a flake
    That the vapour can make
With the moon-tints of purple and pearl,
Can vie with the modest Eulalie's most unregarded curl—
Can compare with the bright-eyed Eulalie's most humble and
    careless curl.

    Now Doubt—now Pain
    Come never again,
For her soul gives me sigh for sigh,
    And all day long
    Shines, bright and strong,
    Astarté within the sky,
While ever to her dear Eulalie upturns her matron eye—
While ever to her young Eulalie upturns her violet eye.

A Valentine

For her this rhyme is penned, whose luminous eyes,
    Brightly expressive as the twins of Loeda,
Shall find her own sweet name, that, nestling lies
    Upon the page, enwrapped from every reader.
Search narrowly the lines!—they hold a treasure
    Divine—a talisman—an amulet
That must be worn *at heart*. Search well the measure—
    The words—the syllables! Do not forget
The trivialest point, or you may lose your labor!
    And yet there is in this no Gordian knot
Which one might not undo without a sabre,
    If one could merely comprehend the plot.

Enwritten upon the leaf where now are peering
 Eyes scintillating soul, there lie *perdus*
Three eloquent words oft uttered in the hearing
 Of poets, by poets—as the name is a poet's, too.
Its letters, although naturally lying
 Like the knight Pinto—Mendez Ferdinando—
Still form a synonym for Truth—Cease trying!
 You will not read the riddle, though you do the best
 you can do.

A Dream Within a Dream

Take this kiss upon the brow!
And, in parting from you now,
Thus much let me avow—
You are not wrong, who deem
That my days have been a dream;
Yet if hope has flown away
In a night, or in a day,
In a vision, or in none,
Is it therefore the less *gone*?
All that we see or seem
Is but a dream within a dream.

I stand amid the roar
Of a surf-tormented shore,
And I hold within my hand
Grains of the golden sand—
How few! yet how they creep
Through my fingers to the deep,
While I weep—while I weep!

O God! can I not grasp
Them with a tighter clasp?
O God! can I not save
One from the pitiless wave?
Is *all* that we see or seem
But a dream within a dream?

Romance

Romance, who loves to nod and sing,
With drowsy head and folded wing,
Among the green leaves as they shake
Far down within some shadowy lake,
To me a painted paroquet
Hath been—a most familiar bird—
Taught me my alphabet to say—
To lisp my very earliest word
While in the wild wood I did lie,
A child—with a most knowing eye.

Of late, eternal Condor years
So shake the very Heaven on high
With tumult as they thunder by,
I have no time for idle cares
Through gazing on the unquiet sky.
And when an hour with calmer wings
Its down upon thy spirit flings—
That little time with lyre and rhyme
To while away—forbidden things!
My heart would feel to be a crime
Unless it trembled with the strings.

To One in Paradise

Thou wast all that to me, love,
    For which my soul did pine—
A green isle in the sea, love,
    A fountain and a shrine,
All wreathed with fairy fruits and flowers,
    And all the flowers were mine.

Ah, dream too bright to last!
    Ah, starry Hope! that didst arise
But to be overcast!
    A voice from out the Future cries,
"On! on!"—but o'er the Past
    (Dim gulf!) my spirit hovering lies
Mute, motionless, aghast!

For, alas! alas! with me
    The light of Life is o'er!
    No more—no more—no more—
(Such language holds the solemn sea
    To the sands upon the shore)
Shall bloom the thunder-blasted tree,
    Or the stricken eagle soar!

And all my days are trances,
    And all my nightly dreams
Are where thy gray eye glances,
    And where thy footstep gleams—
In what ethereal dances,
    By what eternal streams.

ALFRED, LORD TENNYSON
(1809–1892)

It Is the Miller's Daughter

From THE MILLER'S DAUGHTER

It is the miller's daughter,
  And she is grown so dear, so dear,
That I would be the jewel
  That trembles at her ear:
For, hid in ringlets day and night,
I'd touch her neck so warm and white.

And I would be the girdle
  About her dainty, dainty waist,
And her heart would beat against me
  In sorrow and in rest:
And I should know if it beat right,
I'd clasp it round so close and tight.

And I would be the necklace,
  And all day long to fall and rise
Upon her balmy bosom,
  With her laughter or her sighs:
And I would lie so light, so light,
I scarce should be unclasped at night.

Sir Launcelot and Queen Guinevere

Like souls that balance joy and pain,
With tears and smiles from heaven again
The maiden Spring upon the plain
Came in a sun-lit fall of rain.

    In crystal vapor everywhere
Blue isles of heaven laugh'd between,
And far, in forest-deeps unseen,
The topmost elm-tree gather'd green
    From draughts of balmy air.

Sometimes the linnet piped his song;
Sometimes the throstle whistled strong;
Sometimes the sparhawk, wheel'd along,
Hushed all the groves from fear of wrong:
    By grassy capes with fuller sound
In curves the yellowing river ran,
And drooping chestnut-buds began
To spread into the perfect fan,
    Above the teeming ground.

Then, in the boyhood of the year,
Sir Launcelot and Queen Guinevere
Rode thro' the coverts of the deer,
With blissful treble ringing clear.
    She seemed a part of joyous Spring;
A gown of grass-green silk she wore,
Buckled with golden clasps before;
A light-green tuft of plumes she bore
    Closed in a golden ring.

Now on some twisted ivy-net,
Now by some tinkling rivulet,
In mosses mixt with violet
Her cream-white mule his pastern set:
    And fleeter now she skimmed the plains
Than she whose elfin prancer springs
By night to eery warblings,
    When all the glimmering moorland rings
With jingling bridle-reins.

As fast she fled thro' sun and shade,
The happy winds upon her play'd,
Blowing the ringlet from the braid:
She look'd so lovely, as she sway'd
    The rein with dainty finger-tips,
A man had given all other bliss,
And all his worldly worth for this,
To waste his whole heart in one kiss
    Upon her perfect lips.

The Sleeping Beauty

From THE DAY-DREAM

Year after year unto her feet,
   She lying on her couch alone,
Across the purple coverlet,
   The maiden's jet-black hair has grown;
On either side her trancèd form
   Forth streaming from a braid of pearl;

The slumberous light is rich and warm,
   And moves not on the rounded curl.

The silk star-broidered coverlid
   Unto her limbs itself doth mould,
Languidly ever; and amid
   Her full black ringlets, downward rolled,
Glows forth each softly-shadowed arm,
   With bracelets of the diamond bright.
Her constant beauty doth inform
   Stillness with love, and day with light.

She sleeps: her breathings are not heard
   In palace chambers far apart.
The fragrant tresses are not stirred
   That lie upon her charmèd heart.
She sleeps; on either hand upswells
   The gold-fringed pillow lightly prest:
She sleeps, nor dreams, but ever dwells
   A perfect form in perfect rest.

The Arrival

All precious things discovered late,
   To those that seek them issue forth;
For love in sequel works with fate,
   And draws the veil from hidden worth.
He travels far from other skies,
   His mantle glitters on the rocks—
A fairy prince, with joyful eyes,
   And lighter-footed than the fox.

The bodies and the bones of those
   That strove in other days to pass,
Are withered in the thorny close,
   Or scattered blanching in the grass.
He gazes on the silent dead:
   "They perished in their daring deeds."
This proverb flashes through his head:
   "The many fail; the one succeeds."

He comes, scarce knowing what he seeks.
   He breaks the hedge; he enters there;
The color flies into his cheeks;
   He trusts to light on something fair;
For all his life the charm did talk
   About his path, and hover near
With words of promise in his walk,
   And whispered voices in his ear.

More close and close his footsteps wind;
   The magic music in his heart
Beats quick and quicker, till he find
   The quiet chamber far apart.
His spirit flutters like a lark,
   He stoops, to kiss her, on his knee:
"Love, if thy tresses be so dark,
   How dark those hidden eyes must be!"

THE REVIVAL

A touch, a kiss! the charm was snapt.
   There rose a noise of striking clocks,

And feet that ran, and doors that clapt,
    And barking dogs, and crowing cocks;
A fuller light illumined all,
    A breeze through all the garden swept,
A sudden hubbub shook the hall,
    And sixty feet the fountain leapt.

The hedge broke in, the banner blew,
    The butler drank, the steward scrawled,
The fire shot up, the martin flew,
    The parrot screamed, the peacock squalled,
The maid and page renewed their strife,
    The palace banged, and buzzed and clackt,
And all the long-pent stream of life
    Dashed downward in a cataract.

At last with these the king awoke,
    And in his chair himself upreared,
And yawned, and rubbed his face, and spoke,
    "By holy rood, a royal beard!
How say you? we have slept, my lords.
    My beard has grown into my lap."
The barons swore, with many words,
    'T was but an after-dinner's nap.

"Pardy," returned the king, "but still
    My joints are something stiff or so.
My lord, and shall we pass the bill
    I mentioned half an hour ago?"
The chancellor, sedate and vain,
    In courteous words returned reply:

But dallied with his golden chain,
    And, smiling, put the question by.

THE DEPARTURE

And on her lover's arm she leant,
    And round her waist she felt it fold;
And far across the hills they went
    In that new world which is the old.
Across the hills, and far away
    Beyond their utmost purple rim,
And deep into the dying day,
    The happy princess followed him.

"I 'd sleep another hundred years,
    O love, for such another kiss;"
"O wake forever, love," she hears,
    "O love, 't was such as this and this."
And o'er them many a sliding star,
    And many a merry wind was borne,
And, streamed through many a golden bar,
    The twilight melted into morn.

"O eyes long laid in happy sleep!"
    "O happy sleep that lightly fled!"
"O happy kiss, that woke thy sleep!"
    "O love, thy kiss would wake the dead!"
And o'er them many a flowing range
    Of vapor buoyed the crescent bark;
And, rapt thro' many a rosy change,
    The twilight died into the dark.

"A hundred summers! can it be?
    And whither goest thou, tell me where?"
"O, seek my father's court with me,
    For there are greater wonders there."
And o'er the hills, and far away
    Beyond their utmost purple rim,
Beyond the night, across the day,
    Thro' all the world she followed him.

O Swallow, Swallow, Flying South

From THE PRINCESS

O Swallow, Swallow, flying, flying South,
Fly to her, and fall upon her gilded eaves,
And tell her, tell her what I tell to thee.

O tell her, Swallow, thou that knowest each,
That bright and fierce and fickle is the South,
And dark and true and tender is the North.

O Swallow, Swallow, if I could follow, and light
Upon her lattice, I would pipe and trill,
And cheep and twitter twenty million loves.

O were I thou that she might take me in,
And lay me on her bosom, and her heart
Would rock the snowy cradle till I died!

Why lingereth she to clothe her heart with love,
Delaying as the tender ash delays
To clothe herself, when all the woods are green?

O tell her, Swallow, that thy brood is flown:
Say to her, I do but wanton in the South,
But in the North long since my nest is made.

O tell her, brief is life, but love is long,
And brief the sun of summer in the North,
And brief the moon of beauty in the South.

O Swallow, flying from the golden woods,
Fly to her, and pipe and woo her, and make her mine,
And tell her, tell her, that I follow thee.

WILLIAM MAKEPEACE THACKERAY
(1811–1863)

The Age of Wisdom

Ho! pretty page, with the dimpled chin,
  That never has known the barber's shear,
All your wish is woman to win;
This is the way that boys begin—
  Wait till you come to forty year.

Curly gold locks cover foolish brains;
  Billing and cooing is all your cheer;
Sighing, and singing of midnight strains,
Under Bonnybell's window-panes—
  Wait till you come to forty year.

Forty times over let Michaelmas pass;
  Grizzling hair the brain doth clear;
Then you know a boy is an ass,
Then you know the worth of a lass—
  Once you have come to forty year.

Pledge me round; I bid ye declare,
  All good fellows whose beards are gray—
Did not the fairest of the fair
Common grow and wearisome ere
  Ever a month was pass'd away?

The reddest lips that ever have kiss'd,
  The brightest eyes that ever have shone,

May pray and whisper and we not list,
Or look away and never be miss'd—
  Ere yet ever a month is gone.

Gillian's dead! God rest her bier—
  How I loved her twenty years syne!
Marian's married; but I sit here,
Alone and merry at forty year,
  Dipping my nose in the Gascon wine.

ROBERT BROWNING
(1812–1889)

Apparitions

From THE TWO POETS OF CROISIC

Such a starved bank of moss
    Till, that May morn,
Blue ran the flash across:
    Violets were born!

Sky—what a scowl of cloud
    Till, near and far,
Ray on ray split the shroud:
    Splendid, a star!

World—how it walled about
    Life with disgrace
Till God's own smile came out;
    That was thy face!

Meeting at Night

The gray sea, and the long black land;
And the yellow half-moon large and low;
And the startled little waves that leap
In fiery ringlets from their sleep,
As I gain the cove with pushing prow,
And quench its speed i' the slushy sand.

Then a mile of warm, sea-scented beach;
Three fields to cross till a farm appears;
A tap at the pane, the quick sharp scratch
And blue spurt of a lighted match,
And a voice less loud, through its joys and fears,
Than the two hearts, beating each to each.

Wanting Is—What?

    Wanting is—what?
    Summer redundant,
    Blueness abundant,
    —Where is the blot?
Beamy the world, yet a blank all the same,
—Framework which waits for a picture to frame:
What of the leafage, what of the flower?
Roses embowering with naught they embower!
Come then, complete incompletion, O comer,
Pant thro' the blueness, perfect the summer!
        Breathe but one breath
        Rose-beauty above,
        And all that was death
        Grows life, grows love,
            Grows love!

ARTHUR PENRHYN STANLEY
(1815–1881)

Till Death Us Part

"Till death us part,"
  So speaks the heart
When each to each repeats the words of doom;
  For better and for worse,
  Through blessing and through curse,
We will be one, till that dread hour shall come.

  Life with its myriad grasp,
  Our yearning souls shall clasp
By ceaseless love, and still, expectant wonder;
  In bonds that shall endure
  Indissolubly sure
Till God in death shall part our paths asunder.

  Till death us join.
  Oh, word yet more divine!
That to the broken heart breathes hope sublime!
  Through lonely hours,
  And shattered powers,
We still are one, despite of change and time.

  Death, with his healing hand
  Shall knit once more the band,
Which needs but that one link that none may sever;
  Till through the Only Good,
  Heard, felt, and understood,
Our life in God shall make us one forever.

WALT WHITMAN
(1819–1892)

I Am He that Aches with Love

I am he that aches with amorous love;

Does the earth gravitate? does not all matter, aching, attract
all matter?

So the Body of me to all I meet or know.

Once I Pass'd Through a Populous City

Once I pass'd through a populous city imprinting my brain for
future use with its shows, architecture, customs, traditions,

Yet now of all that city I remember only a woman I casually
met there who detain'd me for love of me,

Day by day and night by night we were together—all else
has long been forgotten by me,

I remember I say only that woman who passionately clung
to me,

Again we wander, we love, we separate again,

Again she holds me by the hand, I must not go,

I see her close beside me with silent lips sad and tremulous.

When I Heard at the Close of the Day

When I heard at the close of the day how my name had been
receiv'd with plaudits in the capitol, still it was not a
happy night for me that follow'd,

And else when I carous'd, or when my plans were
accomplish'd, still I was not happy,

But the day when I rose at dawn from the bed of perfect
    health, refresh'd, singing, inhaling the ripe breath of
    autumn,
When I saw the full moon in the west grow pale and
    disappear in the morning light,
When I wander'd alone over the beach, and undressing
    bathed, laughing with the cool waters, and saw the sun
    rise,
And when I thought how my dear friend my lover was on his
    way coming, O then I was happy,
O then each breath tasted sweeter, and all that day my food
    nourish'd me more, and the beautiful day pass'd well,
And the next came with equal joy, and with the next at
    evening came my friend,
And that night while all was still I heard the waters roll slowly
    continually up the shores,
I heard the hissing rustle of the liquid and sands as directed
    to me whispering to congratulate me,
For the one I love most lay sleeping by me under the same
    cover in the cool night,
In the stillness in the autumn moonbeams his face was
    inclined toward me,
And his arm lay lightly around my breast—and that night I
    was happy.

Are You the New Person Drawn Toward Me?

Are you the new person drawn toward me?
To begin with take warning, I am surely far different from
    what you suppose;

Do you suppose you will find in me your ideal?
Do you think it so easy to have me become your lover?
Do you think the friendship of me would be unalloy'd
    satisfaction?
Do you think I am trusty and faithful?
Do you see no further than this façade, this smooth and
    tolerant manner of me?
Do you suppose yourself advancing on real ground toward a
    real heroic man?
Have you no thought O dreamer that it may be all maya,
    illusion?

To a Stranger

Passing stranger! you do not know how longingly I look
    upon you,
You must be he I was seeking, or she I was seeking, (it comes
    to me as of a dream,)
I have somewhere surely lived a life of joy with you,
All is recall'd as we flit by each other, fluid, affectionate,
    chaste, matured,
You grew up with me, were a boy with me or a girl with me,
I ate with you and slept with you, your body has become not
    yours only nor left my body mine only,
You give me the pleasure of your eyes, face, flesh, as we pass,
    you take of my beard, breast, hands, in return,
I am not to speak to you, I am to think of you when I sit
    alone or wake at night alone,
I am to wait, I do not doubt I am to meet you again,
I am to see to it that I do not lose you.

We Two Boys Together Clinging

We two boys together clinging,
One the other never leaving,
Up and down the roads going, North and South excursions
    making,
Power enjoying, elbows stretching, fingers clutching,
Arm'd and fearless, eating, drinking, sleeping, loving,
No law less than ourselves owning, sailing, soldiering,
    thieving, threatening,
Misers, menials, priests alarming, air breathing, water
    drinking, on the turf or the sea-beach dancing,
Cities wrenching, ease scorning, statutes mocking, feebleness
    chasing,
Fulfilling our foray.

I Dream'd in a Dream

I dream'd in a dream I saw a city invincible to the attacks
    of the whole of the rest of the earth,
I dream'd that was the new City of Friends;
Nothing was greater there than the quality of robust
    love—it led the rest,
It was seen every hour in the actions of the men of that city,
And in all their looks and words.

Fast-Anchor'd Eternal O Love!

Fast-anchor'd eternal O love! O woman I love!
O bride! O wife! more resistless than I can tell, the thought of
    you!

Then separate, as disembodied or another born,
Ethereal, the last athletic reality, my consolation,
I ascend, I float in the regions of your love O man,
O sharer of my roving life.

To You

Whoever you are, I fear you are walking the walks of
    dreams,
I fear these supposed realities are to melt from under your
    feet and hands,
Even now your features, joys, speech, house, trade, manners,
    troubles, follies, costume, crimes, dissipate away from
    you,
Your true soul and body appear before me.
They stand forth out of affairs, out of commerce, shops,
    work, farms, clothes, the house, buying, selling, eating,
    drinking, suffering, dying.

Whoever you are, now I place my hand upon you, that you be
    my poem,
I whisper with my lips close to your ear.
I have loved many women and men, but I love none better
    than you.

O I have been dilatory and dumb,
I should have made my way straight to you long ago,
I should have blabb'd nothing but you, I should have chanted
    nothing but you.

I will leave all and come and make the hymns of you,

None has understood you, but I understand you,
None has done justice to you, you have not done justice
    to yourself,
None but has found you imperfect, I only find no
    imperfection in you,
None but would subordinate you, I only am he who will
    never consent to subordinate you,
I only am he who places over you no master, owner, better,
    God, beyond what waits intrinsically in yourself.

Painters have painted their swarming groups and the
    centre-figure of all,
From the head of the centre-figure spreading a nimbus of
    gold-color'd light,
But I paint myriads of heads, but paint no head without its
    nimbus of gold-color'd light,
From my hand from the brain of every man and woman it
    streams, effulgently flowing forever.

O I could sing such grandeurs and glories about you!
You have not known what you are, you have slumber'd
    upon yourself all your life,
Your eyelids have been the same as closed most of the
    time,
What you have done returns already in mockeries,
(Your thrift, knowledge, prayers, if they do not return
    in mockeries, what is their return?)

The mockeries are not you,
Underneath them and within them I see you lurk,
I pursue you where none else has pursued you,

Silence, the desk, the flippant expression, the night, the
    accustom'd routine, if these conceal you from others or
    from yourself, they do not conceal you from me,
The shaved face, the unsteady eye, the impure complexion,
    if these balk others they do not balk me,
The pert apparel, the deform'd attitude, drunkenness, greed,
    premature death, all these I part aside.

There is no endowment in man or woman that is not tallied in
    you,
There is no virtue, no beauty in man or woman, but as good
    is in you,
No pluck, no endurance in others, but as good is in you,
No pleasure waiting for others, but an equal pleasure waits
    for you.

As for me, I give nothing to any one except I give the like
    carefully to you,
I sing the songs of the glory of none, not God, sooner than
    I sing the songs of the glory of you.

Whoever you are! claim your own at any hazard!
These shows of the East and West are tame compared to
    you,
These immense meadows, these interminable rivers, you
    are immense and interminable as they,
These furies, elements, storms, motions of Nature, throes
    of apparent dissolution, you are he or she who is master
    or mistress over them,
Master or mistress in your own right over Nature, elements,
    pain, passion, dissolution.

The hopples fall from your ankles, you find an unfailing
    sufficiency,
Old or young, male or female, rude, low, rejected by the
    rest, whatever you are promulges itself,
Through birth, life, death, burial, the means are provided,
    nothing is scanted,
Through angers, losses, ambition, ignorance, ennui, what you
    are picks its way.

Of Him I Love Day and Night

Of him I love day and night I dream'd I heard he was dead,
And I dream'd I went where they had buried him I love, but
    he was not in that place,
And I dream'd I wander'd searching among burial-places
    to find him,
And I found that every place was a burial-place;
The houses full of life were equally full of death, (this
    house is now,)
The streets, the shipping, the places of amusement, the
    Chicago, Boston, Philadelphia, the Mannahatta, were
    as full of the dead as of the living,
And fuller, O vastly fuller of the dead than of the living;
And what I dream'd I will henceforth tell to every person
    and age,
And I stand henceforth bound to what I dream'd,
And now I am willing to disregard burial-places and
    dispense with them,
And if the memorials of the dead were put up indifferently
    everywhere, even in the room where I eat or sleep, I
    should be satisfied,

And if the corpse of any one I love, or if my own corpse,
    be duly render'd to powder and pour'd in the sea, I
    shall be satisfied,
Or if it be distributed to the winds I shall be satisfied.

As If a Phantom Caress'd Me

As if a phantom caress'd me,
I thought I was not alone walking here by the shore;
But the one I thought was with me as now I walk by the
    shore, the one I loved that caress'd me,
As I lean and look through the glimmering light, that one
    has utterly disappear'd,
And those appear that are hateful to me and mock me.

To One Shortly to Die

From all the rest I single out you, having a message for you,
You are to die—let others tell you what they please, I cannot
    prevaricate,
I am exact and merciless, but I love you—there is no escape
    for you.

Softly I lay my right hand upon you, you just feel it,
I do not argue, I bend my head close and half envelop it,
I sit quietly by, I remain faithful,
I am more than nurse, more than parent or neighbor,
I absolve you from all except yourself spiritual bodily, that
    is eternal, you yourself will surely escape,
The corpse you will leave will be but excrementitious.

The sun bursts through in unlooked-for directions,
Strong thoughts fill you and confidence, you smile,
You forget you are sick, as I forget you are sick,
You do not see the medicines, you do not mind the
     weeping friends, I am with you,
I exclude others from you, there is nothing to be
     commiserated,
I do not commiserate, I congratulate you.

GEORGE ELIOT
(MARY ANNE EVANS)
(1819–1880)

Two Lovers

Two lovers by a moss-grown spring:
They leaned soft cheeks together there,
Mingled the dark and sunny hair,
And heard the wooing thrushes sing.
    O budding time!
    O love's blest prime!

Two wedded from the portal stept:
The bells made happy carolings,
The air was soft as fanning wings,
White petals on the pathway slept.
    O pure-eyed bride!
    O tender pride!

Two faces o'er a cradle bent:
Two hands above the head were locked;
These pressed each other while they rocked,
Those watched a life that love had sent.
    O solemn hour!
    O hidden power!

Two parents by the evening fire:
The red light fell about their knees
On heads that rose by slow degrees
Like buds upon the lily spire.

O patient life!
O tender strife!
The two still sat together there,
The red light shone about their knees;
But all the heads by slow degrees
Had gone and left that lonely pair.
O voyage fast!
O vanished past!

The red light shone upon the floor
And made the space between them wide;
They drew their chairs up side by side,
Their pale cheeks joined, and said,
"Once more!"
O memories!
O past that is!

BAYARD TAYLOR
(1825–1878)

Bedouin Love-Song

From the Desert I come to thee,
  On a stallion shod with fire;
And the winds are left behind
  In the speed of my desire.
Under thy window I stand,
  And the midnight hears my cry:
I love thee, I love but thee!
  With a love that shall not die
    Till the sun grows cold,
    And the stars are old,
    And the leaves of the Judgment
      Book unfold!

Look from thy window, and see
  My passion and my pain!
I lie on the sands below,
  And I faint in thy disdain.
Let the night-winds touch thy brow
  With the heat of my burning sigh,
And melt thee to hear the vow
  Of a love that shall not die
    Till the sun grows cold,
    And the stars are old,
    And the leaves of the Judgment
      Book unfold!

My steps are nightly driven,
　By the fever in my breast,
To hear from thy lattice breathed
　The word that shall give me rest.
Open the door of thy heart,
　And open thy chamber door,
And my kisses shall teach thy lips
　The love that shall fade no more
　　Till the sun grows cold,
　　And the stars are old,
　　And the leaves of the Judgment
　　　Book unfold!

DANTE GABRIEL ROSSETTI
(1828–1882)

Sudden Light

I have been here before,
But when or how I cannot tell:
I know the grass beyond the door,
The sweet keen smell,
The sighing sound, the lights around the shore.

You have been mine before—
How long ago I may not know:
But just when at that swallow's soar
Your neck turn'd so,
Some veil did fall—I knew it all of yore.

Has this been thus before?
And shall not thus time's eddying flight
Still with our lives our love restore
In death's despite,
And day and night yield one delight once more?

When Do I See Thee Most?

From THE HOUSE OF LIFE

When do I see thee most, belovèd one?
When in the light the spirits of mine eyes
Before thy face, their altar, solemnize
The worship of that Love through thee made known?
Or when, in the dusk hours (we two alone),
Close-kissed, and eloquent of still replies
Thy twilight-hidden glimmering visage lies,
And my soul only sees thy soul its own?
O love, my love! if I no more should see
Thyself, nor on the earth the shadow of thee,
Nor image of thine eyes in any spring,—
How then should sound upon Life's darkening slope
The ground-whirl of the perished leaves of Hope,
The wind of Death's imperishable wing!

CHRISTINA ROSSETTI
(1830–1894)

When I Am Dead, My Dearest

When I am dead, my dearest,
Sing no sad songs for me;
Plant thou no roses at my head,
Nor shady cypress tree:
Be the green grass above me
With showers and dewdrops wet;
And if thou wilt, remember,
And if thou wilt, forget.

I shall not see the shadows,
I shall not feel the rain;
I shall not hear the nightingale
Sing on, as if in pain:
And dreaming through the twilight
That doth not rise nor set,
Haply I may remember,
And haply may forget.

EMILY DICKINSON
(1830–1886)

I Had No Time to Hate

I had no time to hate, because
The grave would hinder me,
And life was not so ample I
Could finish enmity.

Nor had I time to love; but since
Some industry must be,
The little toil of love, I thought,
Was large enough for me.

Mine

Mine by the right of the white election!
Mine by the royal seal!
Mine by the sign in the scarlet prison
Bars cannot conceal!

Mine, here in vision and in veto!
Mine, by the grave's repeal
Titled, confirmed—delirious charter!
Mine, while the ages steal!

Bequest

You left me, sweet, two legacies—
A legacy of love

A Heavenly Father would content,
Had He the offer of;

You left me boundaries of pain
Capacious as the sea,
Between eternity and time,
Your consciousness and me.

If You Were Coming in the Fall

If you were coming in the fall,
I'd brush the summer by
With half a smile and half a spurn,
As housewives do a fly.

If I could see you in a year,
I'd wind the months in balls,
And put them each in separate drawers,
Until their time befalls.

If only centuries delayed,
I'd count them on my hand,
Subtracting till my fingers dropped
Into Van Diemen's land.

If certain, when this life was out,
That yours and mine should be,
I'd toss it yonder like a rind,
And taste eternity.

But now, all ignorant of the length
Of time's uncertain wing,
It goads me, like the goblin bee,
That will not state its sting.

With a Flower

I hide myself within my flower,
That wearing on your breast,
You, unsuspecting, wear me too—
And angels know the rest.

I hide myself within my flower,
That, fading from your vase,
You, unsuspecting, feel for me
Almost a loneliness.

Proof

That I did always love,
I bring thee proof:
That till I loved
I did not love enough.

That I shall love alway,
I offer thee
That love is life,
And life hath immortality.

This, dost thou doubt, sweet?
Then have I

Nothing to show
But Calvary.

Have You Got a Brook in Your Little Heart?

Have you got a brook in your little heart,
Where bashful flowers blow,
And blushing birds go down to drink,
And shadows tremble so?

And nobody knows, so still it flows,
That any brook is there;
And yet your little draught of life
Is daily drunken there.

Then look out for the little brook in March,
When the rivers overflow,
And the snows come hurrying from the hills,
And the bridges often go.

And later, in August it may be,
When the meadows parching lie,
Beware, lest this little brook of life
Some burning noon go dry!

Transplanted

As if some little Arctic flower,
Upon the polar hem,
Went wandering down the latitudes,

Until it puzzled came
To continents of summer,
To firmaments of sun,
To strange, bright crowds of flowers,
And birds of foreign tongue!
I say, as if this little flower
To Eden wandered in—
What then? Why, nothing, only,
Your inference therefrom!

The Outlet

My river runs to thee:
Blue sea, wilt welcome me?

My river waits reply.
Oh sea, look graciously!

I'll fetch thee brooks
From spotted nooks,—

Say, sea,
Take me!

In Vain

I cannot live with you,
It would be life,
And life is over there
Behind the shelf

The sexton keeps the key to,
Putting up
Our life, his porcelain,
Like a cup

Discarded of the housewife,
Quaint or broken;
A newer Sevres pleases,
Old ones crack.

I could not die with you,
For one must wait
To shut the other's gaze down—
You could not.

And I, could I stand by
And see you freeze,
Without my right of frost,
Death's privilege?

Nor could I rise with you,
Because your face
Would put out Jesus',
That new grace

Glow plain and foreign
On my homesick eye,
Except that you, than he
Shone closer by.

They'd judge us—how?
For you served Heaven, you know,
Or sought to;
I could not,

Because you saturated sight,
And I had no more eyes
For sordid excellence
As Paradise.

And were you lost, I would be,
Though my name
Rang loudest
On the heavenly fame.

And were you saved,
And I condemned to be
Where you were not,
That self were hell to me.

So we must keep apart,
You there, I here,
With just the door ajar
That oceans are,
And prayer,
And that pale sustenance,
Despair!

Renunciation

There came a day at summer's full
Entirely for me;
I thought that such were for the saints,
Where revelations be.

The sun, as common, went abroad,
The flowers, accustomed, blew,
As if no soul the solstice passed
That maketh all things new.

The time was scarce profaned by speech;
The symbol of a word
Was needless, as at sacrament
The wardrobe of our Lord.

Each was to each the sealed church,
Permitted to commune this time,
Lest we too awkward show
At supper of the Lamb.

The hours slid fast, as hours will,
Clutched tight by greedy hands;
So faces on two decks look back,
Bound to opposing lands.

And so, when all the time had failed,
Without external sound,
Each bound the other's crucifix,
We gave no other bond.

Sufficient troth that we shall rise—
Deposed, at length, the grave—
To that new marriage, justified
Through Calvaries of Love!

Apocalypse

I'm wife; I've finished that,
That other state;
I'm Czar, I'm woman now:
It's safer so.

How odd the girl's life looks
Behind this soft eclipse!
I think that earth seems so
To those in heaven now.

This being comfort, then
That other kind was pain;
But why compare?
I'm wife! stop there!

The Wife

She rose to his requirement, dropped
The playthings of her life
To take the honorable work
Of woman and of wife.

If aught she missed in her new day
Of amplitude, or awe,

Or first prospective, or the gold
In using wore away,

It lay unmentioned, as the sea
Develops pearl and weed,
But only to himself is known
The fathoms they abide.

Apotheosis

Come slowly, Eden!
Lips unused to thee,
Bashful, sip thy jasmines,
As the fainting bee,

Reaching late his flower,
Round her chamber hums,
Counts his nectars—enters,
And is lost in balms!

Choice

Of all the souls that stand create
I have elected one.
When sense from spirit files away,
And subterfuge is done;

When that which is and that which was
Apart, intrinsic, stand,
And this brief tragedy of flesh
Is shifted like a sand;

When figures show their royal front
And mists are carved away,—
Behold the atom I preferred
To all the lists of clay!

I Have No Life but This

I have no life but this,
To lead it here;
Nor any death, but lest
Dispelled from there;

Nor tie to earths to come,
Nor action new,
Except through this extent,
The realm of you.

The Contract

I gave myself to him,
And took himself for pay.
The solemn contract of a life
Was ratified this way.

The wealth might disappoint,
Myself a poorer prove
Than this great purchaser suspect,
The daily own of Love

Depreciate the vision;
But, till the merchant buy,

Still fable, in the isles of spice,
The subtle cargoes lie.

At least, 'tis mutual risk—
Some found it mutual gain;
Sweet debt of Life—each night to owe,
Insolvent, every noon.

Wild Nights

Wild nights! Wild nights!
Were I with thee,
Wild nights should be
Our luxury!

Futile the winds
To a heart in port—
Done with the compass,
Done with the chart.

Rowing in Eden!
Ah! the sea!
Might I but moor
To-night in thee!

Possession

Did the harebell loose her girdle
To the lover bee,
Would the bee the harebell hallow
Much as formerly?

Did the paradise, persuaded,
Yield her moat of pearl,
Would the Eden be an Eden,
Or the earl an earl?

The Lovers

The rose did caper on her cheek,
Her bodice rose and fell,
Her pretty speech, like drunken men,
Did stagger pitiful.

Her fingers fumbled at her work—
Her needle would not go;
What ailed so smart a little maid
It puzzled me to know,

Till opposite I spied a cheek
That bore another rose;
Just opposite, another speech
That like the drunkard goes;

A vest that, like the bodice, danced
To the immortal tune—
Till those two troubled little clocks
Ticked softly into one.

In Lands I Never Saw, They Say

In lands I never saw, they say,
Immortal Alps look down,
Whose bonnets touch the firmament,
Whose sandals touch the town—

Meek at whose everlasting feet
A myriad daisies play.
Which, sir, are you, and which am I,
Upon an August day?

The Moon Is Distant from the Sea

The moon is distant from the sea,
And yet with amber hands
She leads him, docile as a boy,
Along appointed sands.

He never misses a degree;
Obedient to her eye,
He comes just so far toward the town,
Just so far goes away.

Oh, Signor, thine the amber hand,
And mine the distant sea—
Obedient to the least command
Thine eyes impose on me.

The Lost Jewel

I held a jewel in my fingers
And went to sleep.
The day was warm, and winds were prosy;
I said: " 'Twill keep."

I woke and chid my honest fingers—
The gem was gone;
And now an amethyst remembrance
Is all I own.

What if I Say I Shall Not Wait?

What if I say I shall not wait?
What if I burst the fleshly gate
And pass, escaped, to thee?
What if I file this mortal off,
See where it hurt me—that's enough—
And wade in liberty?

They cannot take us any more—
Dungeons may call, and guns implore;
Unmeaning now, to me,
As laughter was an hour ago,
Or laces, or a travelling show,
Or who died yesterday!

Love

Love is anterior to life,
  Posterior to death,
Initial of creation, and
  The exponent of breath.

With a Flower

When roses cease to bloom, dear,
  And violets are done,
When bumble-bees in solemn flight
  Have passed beyond the sun,

The hand that paused to gather
  Upon this summer's day
Will idle lie, in Auburn,—
  Then take my flower, pray!

Song

Summer for thee grant I may be
  When summer days are flown!
Thy music still when whippoorwill
  And oriole are done!

For thee to bloom, I'll skip the tomb
  And sow my blossoms o'er!
Pray gather me, Anemone,
  Thy flower forevermore!

Loyalty

Split the lark and you'll find the music,
  Bulb after bulb, in silver rolled,
Scantily dealt to the summer morning,
  Saved for your ear when lutes be old.

Loose the flood, you shall find it patent,
  Gush after gush, reserved for you;
Scarlet experiment! sceptic Thomas,
  Now, do you doubt that your bird was true?

To Lose Thee, Sweeter than to Gain

To lose thee, sweeter than to gain
  All other hearts I knew.
'Tis true the drought is destitute,
  But then I had the dew!

The Caspian has its realms of sand,
  Its other realm of sea;
Without the sterile perquisite
  No Caspian could be.

Poor Little Heart

Poor little heart!
Did they forget thee?
Then dinna care! Then dinna care!

Proud little heart!
Did they forsake thee?
Be debonair! Be debonair!

Frail little heart!
I would not break thee:
Could'st credit me? Could'st credit me?

Gay little heart!
Like morning glory
Thou'll wilted be; thou'll wilted be!

I've Got an Arrow Here

I've got an arrow here;
Loving the hand that sent it,
I the dart revere.

Fell, they will say, in "skirmish"!
Vanquished, my soul will know,
By but a simple arrow
Sped by an archer's bow.

The Master

He fumbles at your spirit
As players at the keys
Before they drop full music on;
He stuns you by degrees,

Prepares your brittle substance
  For the ethereal blow,
By fainter hammers, further heard,
  Then nearer, then so slow

Your breath has time to straighten,
  Your brain to bubble cool—
Deals one imperial thunderbolt
  That scalps your naked soul.

Heart, We Will Forget Him

Heart, we will forget him!
  You and I, tonight!
You may forget the warmth he gave,
  I will forget the light.

When you have done, pray tell me,
  That I my thoughts may dim;
Haste! lest while you're lagging,
  I may remember him!

We Outgrow Love Like Other Things

We outgrow love like other things
  And put it in the drawer,
Till it an antique fashion shows
  Like costumes grandsires wore.

Not with a Club the Heart Is Broken

Not with a club the heart is broken,
    Nor with a stone;
A whip, so small you could not see it,
    I've known

To lash the magic creature
    Till it fell,
Yet that whip's name too noble
    Then to tell.

Magnanimous of bird
    By boy descried,
To sing unto the stone
    Of which it died.

Numen Lumen

I live with him, I see his face;
  I go no more away
For visitor, or sundown;
  Death's single privacy,

The only one forestalling mine,
  And that by right that he
Presents a claim invisible,
  No wedlock granted me.

I live with him, I hear his voice,
  I stand alive to-day

To witness to the certainty
  Of immortality

Taught me by Time—the lower way,
  Conviction every day—
That life like this is endless,
  Be judgment what it may.

Longing

I envy seas whereon he rides,
  I envy spokes of wheels
Of chariots that him convey,
  I envy speechless hills

That gaze upon his journey;
  How easy all can see
What is forbidden utterly
  As heaven, unto me!

I envy nests of sparrows
  That dot his distant eaves,
The wealthy fly upon his pane,
  The happy, happy leaves

That just abroad his window
  Have summer's leave to be,
The earrings of Pizarro
  Could not obtain for me.

I envy light that wakes him,
  And bells that boldly ring
To tell him it is noon abroad—
  Myself his noon could bring,

Yet interdict my blossom
  And abrogate my bee,
Lest noon in everlasting night
  Drop Gabriel and me.

JAMES WHITCOMB RILEY
(1849–1916)

An Old Sweetheart of Mine

As one who cons at evening o'er an album all alone,
And muses on the faces of the friends that he has known,
So I turn the leaves of fancy, till in shadowy design
I find the smiling features of an old sweetheart of mine.

The lamplight seems to glimmer with a flicker of surprise,
As I turn it low to rest me of the dazzle in my eyes,
And light my pipe in silence, save a sigh that seems to yoke
Its fate with my tobacco, and to vanish with the smoke.

'T is a fragrant retrospection—for the loving thoughts that
    start
Into being are like perfume from the blossom of the heart;
And to dream the old dreams over is a luxury divine—
When my truant fancy wanders with that old sweetheart of
    mine.

Though I hear, beneath my study, like a fluttering of wings,
The voices of my children, and the mother as she sings,
I feel no twinge of conscience to deny me any theme
When Care has cast her anchor in the harbor of a dream.

In fact, to speak in earnest, I believe it adds a charm
To spice the good a trifle with a little dust of harm—
For I find an extra flavor in Memory's mellow wine
That makes me drink the deeper to that old sweetheart of mine.

A face of lily-beauty, with a form of airy grace,
Floats out of my tobacco as the genii from the vase;
And I thrill beneath the glances of a pair of azure eyes
As glowing as the summer and as tender as the skies.

I can see the pink sunbonnet and the little checkered dress
She wore when first I kissed her and she answered the caress
With the written declaration that, "as surely as the vine
Grew round the stump," she loved me—that old sweetheart
    of mine.

And again I feel the pressure of her slender little hand,
As we used to talk together of the future we had planned—
When I should be a poet, and with nothing else to do
But write the tender verses that she set the music to:

When we should live together in a cosy little cot,
Hid in a nest of roses, with a fairy garden-spot,
Where the vines were ever fruited, and the weather ever fine,
And the birds were ever singing for that old sweetheart of
    mine:

When I should be her lover forever and a day,
And she my faithful sweetheart till the golden hair was gray;
And we should be so happy that when either's lips were dumb
They would not smile in Heaven till the other's kiss had come.

But, ah! my dream is broken by a step upon the stair,
And the door is softly opened, and—my wife is standing there;
Yet with eagerness and rapture all my visions I resign
To greet the living presence of that old sweetheart of mine.

OSCAR WILDE
(1854–1900)

Requiescat

Tread lightly, she is near
  Under the snow,
Speak gently, she can hear
  The daisies grow.

All her bright golden hair
  Tarnished with rust,
She that was young and fair
  Fallen to dust.

Lily-like, white as snow,
  She hardly knew
She was a woman, so
  Sweetly she grew.

Coffin-board, heavy stone,
  Lie on her breast,
I vex my heart alone,
  She is at rest.

Peace, Peace, she cannot hear
  Lyre or sonnet,
All my life's buried here,
  Heap earth upon it.

PAKENHAM BEATTY
(1855–1930)

When Will Love Come?

Some find Love late, some find him soon,
  Some with the rose in May,
Some with the nightingale in June,
  And some when skies are gray;
Love comes to some with smiling eyes,
  And comes with tears to some;
For some Love sings, for some Love sighs,
  For some Love's lips are dumb.
How will you come to me, fair Love?
  Will you come late or soon?
With sad or smiling skies above,
  By light of sun or moon?
Will you be sad, will you be sweet,
  Sing, sigh, Love, or be dumb?
Will it be summer when we meet,
  Or autumn ere you come?

WILLIAM BUTLER YEATS
(1865–1939)

He Wishes for the Cloths of Heaven

Had I the heavens' embroidered cloths,
Enwrought with golden and silver light,
The blue and the dim and the dark cloths
Of night and light and the half light,
I would spread the cloths under your feet:
But I, being poor, have only my dreams;
I have spread my dreams under your feet;
Tread softly because you tread on my dreams.

When You Are Old

When you are old and grey and full of sleep,
And nodding by the fire, take down this book,
And slowly read, and dream of the soft look
Your eyes had once, and of their shadows deep;

How many loved your moments of glad grace,
And loved your beauty with love false or true,
But one man loved the pilgrim soul in you,
And loved the sorrows of your changing face;

And bending down beside the glowing bars,
Murmur, a little sadly, how Love fled
And paced upon the mountains overhead
And hid his face amid a crowd of stars.

To a Young Girl

My dear, my dear, I know
More than another
What makes your heart beat so;
Not even your own mother
Can know it as I know,
Who broke my heart for her
When the wild thought,
That she denies
And has forgot,
Set all her blood astir
And glittered in her eyes.

AMY LOWELL

(1874–1925)

Patterns

I walk down the garden-paths,
And all the daffodils
Are blowing, and the bright blue squills.
I walk down the patterned garden-paths
In my stiff, brocaded gown.
With my powdered hair and jewelled fan,
I too am a rare
Pattern. As I wander down
The garden-paths.

My dress is richly figured,
And the train
Makes a pink and silver stain
On the gravel, and the thrift
Of the borders.
Just a plate of current fashion,
Tripping by in high-heeled, ribboned shoes.
Not a softness anywhere about me,
Only whalebone and brocade.
And I sink on a seat in the shade
Of a lime-tree. For my passion
Wars against the stiff brocade.
The daffodils and squills
Flutter in the breeze
As they please.

And I weep;
For the lime-tree is in blossom
And one small flower has dropped upon my bosom.

And the plashing of waterdrops
In the marble fountain
Comes down the garden-paths.
The dripping never stops.
Underneath my stiffened gown
Is the softness of a woman bathing in a marble basin,
A basin in the midst of hedges grown
So thick, she cannot see her lover hiding,
But she guesses he is near,
And the sliding of the water
Seems the stroking of a dear
Hand upon her.
What is Summer in a fine brocaded gown!
I should like to see it lying in a heap upon the ground.
All the pink and silver crumpled up on the ground.

I would be the pink and silver as I ran along the paths,
And he would stumble after,
Bewildered by my laughter.
I should see the sun flashing from his sword-hilt and the
    buckles on his shoes.
I would choose
To lead him in a maze along the patterned paths,
A bright and laughing maze for my heavy-booted lover,
Till he caught me in the shade,
And the buttons of his waistcoat bruised my body as he
    clasped me,

Aching, melting, unafraid.
With the shadows of the leaves and the sundrops,
And the plopping of the waterdrops,
All about us in the open afternoon—
I am very like to swoon
With the weight of this brocade,
For the sun sifts through the shade.

Underneath the fallen blossom
In my bosom,
Is a letter I have hid.
It was brought to me this morning by a rider from the
      Duke.
"Madam, we regret to inform you that Lord Hartwell
Died in action Thursday sen'night."
As I read it in the white, morning sunlight,
The letters squirmed like snakes.
"Any answer, Madam," said my footman.
"No," I told him.
"See that the messenger takes some refreshment.
No, no answer."
And I walked into the garden,
Up and down the patterned paths,
In my stiff, correct brocade.
The blue and yellow flowers stood up proudly in the sun,
Each one.
I stood upright too,
Held rigid to the pattern
By the stiffness of my gown.
Up and down I walked,
Up and down.

In a month he would have been my husband.
In a month, here, underneath this lime,
We would have broke the pattern;
He for me, and I for him,
He as Colonel, I as Lady,
On this shady seat.
He had a whim
That sunlight carried blessing.
And I answered, "It shall be as you have said."
Now he is dead.

In Summer and in Winter I shall walk
Up and down
The patterned garden-paths
In my stiff, brocaded gown.
The squills and daffodils
Will give place to pillared roses, and to asters, and
    to snow.
I shall go
Up and down,
In my gown.
Gorgeously arrayed,
Boned and stayed.
And the softness of my body will be guarded from
    embrace
By each button, hook, and lace.
For the man who should loose me is dead,
Fighting with the Duke in Flanders,
In a pattern called a war.
Christ! What are patterns for?

ROBERT FROST
(1874–1963)

Wind and Window Flower

Lovers, forget your love,
    And list to the love of these,
She a window flower,
    And he a winter breeze.

When the frosty window veil
    Was melted down at noon,
And the cagèd yellow bird
    Hung over her in tune,

He marked her through the pane,
    He could not help but mark,
And only passed her by,
    To come again at dark.

He was a winter wind,
    Concerned with ice and snow,
Dead weeds and unmated birds,
    And little of love could know.

But he sighed upon the sill,
    He gave the sash a shake,
As witness all within
    Who lay that night awake.

Perchance he half prevailed
    To win her for the flight
From the firelit looking-glass
    And warm stove-window light.

But the flower leaned aside
    And thought of naught to say,
And morning found the breeze
    A hundred miles away.

Flower-gathering

I left you in the morning,
And in the morning glow,
You walked a way beside me
To make me sad to go.
Do you know me in the gloaming,
Gaunt and dusty grey with roaming?
Are you dumb because you know me not,
Or dumb because you know?

All for me? And not a question
For the faded flowers gay
That could take me from beside you
For the ages of a day?
They are yours, and be the measure
Of their worth for you to treasure,
The measure of the little while
That I've been long away.

To Earthward

Love at the lips was touch
As sweet as I could bear;
And once that seemed too much;
I lived on air

That crossed me from sweet things,
The flow of—was it musk
From hidden grapevine springs
Down hill at dusk?

I had the swirl and ache
From sprays of honeysuckle
That when they're gathered shake
Dew on the knuckle.

I craved strong sweets, but those
Seemed strong when I was young;
The petal of the rose
It was that stung.

Now no joy but lacks salt
That is not dashed with pain
And weariness and fault;
I crave the stain

Of tears, the aftermark
Of almost too much love,
The sweet of bitter bark
And burning clove.

When stiff and sore and scarred
I take away my hand
From leaning on it hard
In grass and sand,

The hurt is not enough:
I long for weight and strength
To feel the earth as rough
To all my length.

ANGELA MORGAN

(c. 1875–1957)

Choice

I'd rather have the thought of you
To hold against my heart,
My spirit to be taught of you
With west winds blowing,
Than all the warm caresses
Of another love's bestowing,
Or all the glories of the world
In which you had no part.

I'd rather have the theme of you
To thread my nights and days,
I'd rather have the dream of you
With faint stars glowing,
I'd rather have the want of you,
The rich, elusive taunt of you
Forever and forever and forever unconfessed
Than claim the alien comfort
Of any other's breast.

O lover! O my lover,
That this should come to me!
I'd rather have the hope for you,
Ah, Love, I'd rather grope for you
Within the great abyss
Than claim another's kiss—
Alone I'd rather go my way
Throughout eternity.

CARL SANDBURG
(1878–1967)

A Dream Girl

You will come one day in a waver of love,
Tender as dew, impetuous as rain,
The tan of the sun will be on your skin,
The purr of the breeze in your murmuring speech,
You will pose with a hill-flower grace.

You will come, with your slim, expressive arms,
A poise of the head no sculptor has caught
And nuances spoken with shoulder and neck,
Your face in a pass-and-repass of moods
As many as skies in delicate change
Of cloud and blue and flimmering sun.

      Yet,
You may not come, O girl of a dream,
We may but pass as the world goes by
And take from a look of eyes into eyes,
A film of hope and a memoried day.

ALFRED NOYES
(1880–1958)

The Highwayman

PART ONE

I

The wind was a torrent of darkness among the gusty trees,
The moon was a ghostly galleon tossed upon cloudy seas,
The road was a ribbon of moonlight over the purple moor,
And the highwayman came riding—
    Riding—riding—
The highwayman came riding, up to the old inn-door.

II

He'd a French cocked-hat on his forehead, a bunch of lace at
    his chin,
A coat of the claret velvet, and breeches of brown doe-skin;
They fitted with never a wrinkle: his boots were up to the
    thigh!
And he rode with a jewelled twinkle,
    His pistol butts a-twinkle,
His rapier hilt a-twinkle, under the jewelled sky.

III

Over the cobbles he clattered and clashed in the dark inn-yard,
And he tapped with his whip on the shutters, but all was
    locked and barred;
He whistled a tune to the window, and who should be waiting
    there

But the landlord's black-eyed daughter,
 Bess, the landlord's daughter,
Plaiting a dark red love-knot into her long black hair.

IV

And dark in the dark old inn-yard a stable-wicket creaked
Where Tim the ostler listened; his face was white and peaked;
His eyes were hollows of madness, his hair like mouldy hay,
But he loved the landlord's daughter,
 The landlord's red-lipped daughter,
Dumb as a dog he listened, and he heard the robber say—

V

"One kiss, my bonny sweetheart, I'm after a prize to-night,
But I shall be back with the yellow gold before the morning
 light;
Yet, if they press me sharply, and harry me through the day,
Then look for me by moonlight,
 Watch for me by moonlight,
I'll come to thee by moonlight, though hell should bar the way."

VI

He rose upright in the stirrups; he scarce could reach her hand,
But she loosened her hair i' the casement! His face burnt like
 a brand
As the black cascade of perfume came tumbling over his
 breast;
And he kissed its waves in the moonlight,
 (Oh, sweet black waves in the moonlight!)
Then he tugged at his rein in the moonlight, and galloped
 away to the West.

PART TWO

I

He did not come in the dawning; he did not come at noon;
And out o' the tawny sunset, before the rise o' the moon,
When the road was a gipsy's ribbon, looping the purple moor,
A red-coat troop came marching—
    Marching—marching—
King George's men came marching, up to the old inn-door.

II

They said no word to the landlord, they drank his ale instead,
But they gagged his daughter and bound her to the foot of
    her narrow bed;
Two of them knelt at her casement, with muskets at their side!
There was death at every window;
    And hell at one dark window;
For Bess could see, through her casement, the road that *he*
    would ride.

III

They had tied her up to attention, with many a sniggering
    jest;
They had bound a musket beside her, with the barrel beneath
    her breast!
"Now keep good watch!" and they kissed her.
She heard the dead man say—
Look for me by moonlight;
    Watch for me by moonlight;
I'll come to thee by moonlight, though hell should bar the way!

IV

She twisted her hands behind her; but all the knots held good!
She writhed her hands till her fingers were wet with sweat or
    blood!
They stretched and strained in the darkness, and the hours
    crawled by like years,
Till, now, on the stroke of midnight,
    Cold, on the stroke of midnight,
The tip of one finger touched it! The trigger at least was hers!

V

The tip of one finger touched it; she strove no more for the
    rest!
Up, she stood up to attention, with the barrel beneath her
    breast,
She would not risk their hearing; she would not strive again;
For the road lay bare in the moonlight;
    Blank and bare in the moonlight;
And the blood of her veins in the moonlight throbbed to her
    love's refrain.

VI

Tlot-tlot; tlot-tlot! Had they heard it? The horse-hoofs ringing
    clear;
Tlot-tlot, tlot-tlot, in the distance? Were they deaf that they
    did not hear?
Down the ribbon of moonlight, over the brow of the hill,
The highwayman came riding,
    Riding, riding!
The red-coats looked to their priming! She stood up, straight
    and still!

VII

Tlot-tlot, in the frosty silence! *Tlot-tlot*, in the echoing night!
Nearer he came and nearer! Her face was like a light!
Her eyes grew wide for a moment; she drew one last deep
    breath,
Then her finger moved in the moonlight,
    Her musket shattered the moonlight,
Shattered her breast in the moonlight and warned him—with
    her death.

VIII

He turned; he spurred to the West; he did not know who
    stood
Bowed, with her head o'er the musket, drenched with her
    own red blood!
Not till the dawn he heard it, his face grew grey to hear
How Bess, the landlord's daughter,
    The landlord's black-eyed daughter,
Had watched for her love in the moonlight, and died in the
    darkness there.

IX

Back, he spurred like a madman, shrieking a curse to the sky,
With the white road smoking behind him and his rapier
    brandished high!
Blood-red were his spurs i' the golden noon; wine-red was
    his velvet coat,
When they shot him down on the highway,
    Down like a dog on the highway,
And he lay in his blood on the highway, with the bunch of
    lace at his throat.

X

And still of a winter's night, they say, when the wind is in the
    trees,
When the moon is a ghostly galleon tossed upon cloudy seas,
When the road is a ribbon of moonlight over the purple moor,
A highwayman comes riding—
    Riding—riding—
A highwayman comes riding, up to the old inn-door.

XI

Over the cobbles he clatters and clangs in the dark inn-yard;
He taps with his whip on the shutters, but all is locked and barred;
He whistles a tune to the window, and who should be waiting
    there
But the landlord's black-eyed daughter,
    Bess, the landlord's daughter,
Plaiting a dark red love-knot into her long black hair.

SARA TEASDALE
(1884–1933)

I Am Not Yours

I am not yours, not lost in you,
Not lost, although I long to be
Lost as a candle lit at noon,
Lost as a snowflake in the sea.

You love me, and I find you still
A spirit beautiful and bright,
Yet I am I, who long to be
Lost as a light is lost in light.

Oh plunge me deep in love—put out
My senses, leave me deaf and blind,
Swept by the tempest of your love,
A taper in a rushing wind.

May

The wind is tossing the lilacs,
The new leaves laugh in the sun,
And the petals fall on the orchard wall,
But for me the spring is done.

Beneath the apple blossoms
I go a wintry way,
For love that smiled in April
Is false to me in May.

The Kiss

I hoped that he would love me,
And he has kissed my mouth,
But I am like a stricken bird
That cannot reach the south.

For though I know he loves me,
To-night my heart is sad;
His kiss was not so wonderful
As all the dreams I had.

Word Cloud Classics

Adventures of Huckleberry Finn

The Adventures of Sherlock Holmes

Aesop's Fables

*Alice's Adventures in Wonderland
and Through the Looking-Glass*

Anna Karenina

Anne of Green Gables

The Art of War

The Awakening and Other Stories

*The Beautiful and Damned
and Other Stories*

The Brothers Grimm 101 Fairy Tales

*The Brothers Grimm Volume II:
110 Grimmer Fairy Tales*

Classic Horror Tales

Classic Westerns: Zane Grey

The Count of Monte Cristo

Crime and Punishment

Frankenstein

Hans Christian Andersen Tales

*H. P. Lovecraft Cthulhu
Mythos Tales*

*The Inventions, Researches, and
Writings of Nikola Tesla*

The Jungle Book

Leaves of Grass

Les Misérables

My Ántonia

*Narrative of the Life of Frederick
Douglass and Other Works*

Odyssey

Peter Pan

The Phantom of the Opera

The Picture of Dorian Gray

Pride and Prejudice

The Romantic Poets

*Selected Works of
Alexander Hamilton*

Sense and Sensibility

*Shakespeare's Sonnets and
Other Poems*

Treasure Island

*Uncle Tom's Cabin, or Life
Among the Lowly*

*The Wind in the Willows
and Other Stories*

The Wizard of Oz

Wuthering Heights

For more titles, please visit our website:
www.canterburyclassicsbooks.com